I0579476

Dirty Laundry

Aster(ix) Journal

presents

Dirty Laundry

Fall 2017

Edited by
Angie Cruz,
and Adriana E. Ramírez

BLUE SKETCH PRESS | PITTSBURGH

See page 125 for individual copyright information/acknowledgments.

Published via Blue Sketch Press, Pittsburgh.
www.bluesketchpress.com

Dirty Laundry: An Aster(ix) Anthology / Aster(ix) Journal
Edited by Angie Cruz & Adriana E. Ramírez—1st ed.
ISBN (print) 978-1-942547-08-2 (trade paperback)
1-942547-08-2 (ISBN-10)
Cover Design by Little Owl Creative. Cover image by Erika Morillo.
Copy-Edited by Joseph N. Welch III.

First Edition: December 2017

Printed in the United States of America
9 8 7 6 5 4 3 2 1

Aster(ix) Journal
www.asterixjournal.com

Aster(ix) is usually published 2-3 times a year in print with additional content online.

Funded in part by the Dietrich School of Arts and Sciences and the Department of English at University of Pittsburgh.

Contents

A Note from the Editors

Angie Cruz & Adriana E. Ramírez

"Go away!

I want to look at myself.

To look at myself in my own light." Marigloria Palma

Translated by Carina del Valle Schorske

Angie Cruz: Maybe we should start with the fact that this issue was anchored by a conversation we had with Sandra Cisneros when she visited Pittsburgh, and she spontaneously had us draw maps at the dinner table. How we quickly could see by looking at our maps where we have been and even where we wanted to go. Some of us were very good at it, some of us couldn't barely orient the cities we live in. We understood it was a rare occasion, eight Latino/as, all writers at different stages of our careers, all very much committed to making this world a better place. I think this conversation is the heart of the issue. Maybe we didn't have it in mind directly when we went through the submissions, but as we made our choices, we realized all the pieces aired some dirty laundry. All the pieces in some way share an intimacy between women, between fathers and sons, lovers, friends, mothers and daughters. All swing open the door and allow us into the devastation of loss, what we desire, what we are capable of. Don't you think?

Adriana E. Ramírez: Absolutely! One of the things I love about the phrase "la ropa sucia se lava en casa," is that there is an inherent contradiction to it—when I think of dirty clothes, I imagine laundry lines, with all the linens on display. Yet, the way the phrase is used, dirty clothes are meant to be hidden, obscured—the mystery preserved. I think this tension/contradiction is helpful, even going back to our maps. Mine was so detailed—anally correct, even. I felt the need to hide it, afterwards. Because there was a shame in being so exact, so nerdy, so eager to show off what I knew. Other people at the table did the opposite. Only three states would be labeled, but the person describing the drawing would boast of their lack of knowledge, root their minimal geographical knowledge in a story, a personal history. Being a little wrong cartographically didn't matter, what mattered was the story. Hence, my shame at hiding my perfectly crisp and white laundry—there's no story there. I wanted the story. That mood, the desire for the imperfect but powerful histories we carry, informed this issue, from that dinner to the final edits we're making as we write this!

AC: The best part of collaborating on this issue with you is that, even if we work together on Aster(ix), we don't always have time to share or talk in depth about what we love in writing. So I loved rereading pieces that "slayed" you, as you said about Norma Liliana Valdez's poems. I love that poem too, but I wonder why that one hit you so hard.

AER: I've been wanting to write that poem for years. I'd read a story in the newspaper about twenty people found in a shipping container in the desert. Their bodies and stories haunted me. And I'd been trying to figure out how to write a poem that carried that weight, both in scarcity of language and power of feeling. I've thrown out dozens of drafts. And then, reading Valdez's poem, I knew I could stop trying.

She'd done it so perfectly, so beautifully. The simplicity of the image, the connotations of grief and life in the final line. Some poems punch you in the gut in the best way possible. This one slapped me in the face. And I'm better for it.

AC: In our conversation, Sandra mentioned Joe Jimenez as a writer she loved—so of course I reached out to him to solicit some of his work. When he sent us his essay, I was completely unhinged by it. He wrote, "There are stories I am not going to tell you," and then "In other words, maybe it's the guilt I will forever carry when I watched and did nothing as my mom's boyfriend and his friends beat the shit out of an opossum with a baseball bat." I think the issue is filled with that tension between what we are not allowed to say, what we fear to say, what we will say anyway.

AER: And what we can't say, even if we want to. Absolutely. Jimenez's piece is a delicate dance—tough to execute correctly (as are all lyric essays). I admire the pacing in particular, the breaths between verses. I think that silence speaks to the heart of what you're saying. Is that silence driven by fear? By rule? By choice?

AC: In "The Algorithm Falters," Galaviz writes, "The boy on Match doesn't ask what you want, but we are getting more accustomed to this, to speaking even when we aren't invited to, because we so rarely are." In this #metoo moment I find that many of these stories—from Alvarez's "Swinging from A Chandelier," that resists the conventions of being a married women, to Huerta's character's embrace of the bruja gift her mother passed on to her—are a way of speaking up, of complicating what women are capable of and who we are.

AER: Those complications are my favorite part—those are the things that stick with you, long after you've put the pages down.

How to Search For Your Child

Norma Liliana Valdez

Colinas de Santa Fe, Veracruz, México

Drive a six-foot metal rod into the ground.
With each click-clack of the hammer,
dig the cross-shaped bar deeper into the soil.
Pull out the rod.
Bring it close to your nose.
Inhale. Wet earth or remains?
Exhume 253 bodies, none of them yours.
Yellow your skin.
Grow your hair waist-length.

Tlaquaches

Joe Jiménez

i.

I don't recall the first time I saw a tlaquache, an opossum, though I do remember the first memory I carry of one. Tucked inside me, an assemblage of ideas behind my heart, maybe, or just under it, left in that dry dirt, in the weeds of things I do not like to think about but, even with effort, cannot forget. An alley, maybe a monte, an abandoned lot, a room, maybe a shed or a pouch, a field of dark mud, some realm inside us that shoulders our shadows—I think each of us carries such a place.

In the summer, after wanting very badly to, I read the opening to Édouard Louis's *The End of Eddy*, and I remembered, then, horribly, while laying in my bed, while cuddling my small hairless dog, who died at the end of that summer, I remembered my mother's boyfriend, and I remembered that small opossum on the fence one night when I was very young, and I remembered the baseball bat, a man's bulging brown arm, the look of bonecrush and gutcry, the grown man's full-muscled swings.

In the opening of Louis's novel, we are told about the boy's father and we are told about their poverty and their hardships and his queerness growing up in a small French town, and I remember all of this, having identified very much with its shadows, even if my own life came about half a world away. We are told that the boy himself is soft in the ways that boys like us can be soft, and also, we are told the boy's father is cruel, an attribute, a behavior, a routine proven so early in the novel by the father's resolution to his problem of the stray cat that stayed near the house having kittens. So early in that story, Louis tells us the father places the stray's kittens in a plastic bag and slams the bag, the bag with small kittens inside it, against the brick wall. Again, again, he does this. Again, again, he kills them. Until there were no more cries. A resolution, perhaps for the father, ridding himself of these kittens. Yet, resolution for someone often leads to irresolution for another—as it so often plays out, someone's light is ultimately someone else's great darkness.

I do not have to tell you my mom's boyfriend was a real asshole; I do not have to tell you all the shit things he did to my family. But I will tell you that all of the world is stark naked—it is, at some point, when no one or when everyone is watching.

Yes, that night, I saw men kill a tlaquache. Yes, they used a baseball bat. Yes, it was brutal. Those men laughed and they laughed, yes. I was twelve, thirteen, maybe. A strange place, that age, that place of a boy's life, with the children in the bedroom playing a game and the women around the table laughing and laughing, swallowing their beer, and the men being men in the trees under the streetlights, their long tongues, their sweat, like their stories, building lies of the real men they were and how each, via his tale, held membership in the clan.

Afterward, away from them, behind my mom's boyfriend's grey truck parked on the street, when no one was watching, I squatted down to my knees, and holding my fists over my eyes, I imagined what had happened to the small opossum's body, which lay, then, on the other side of the fence, in an alley, where they'd pitched its battered body when they were done with it. I felt something in my throat, my curled heart. In my heart, a heat I've encountered only a few other times in my life. Call it rage, call it clarity, call it brownness and queerness. And while I could hear them joking near the barbecue pit, I tried not to think of it, and I promised myself I would grow stronger than them all one day—with my heart in my mouth, I tried not to think of taking a baseball bat to each one of those shitty men.

ii.

I cannot say that I have always loved tlaquaches. They are not like hummingbirds or jaguars—there is no glamor to a tlaquache. Hummingbirds are magical, of course. The fury of their marvelous wings, their iridescent green coats, their red throats. Jaguars, also, with their magnificence, their predatory prowess, their status as warrior symbol, are easy to love or fear, maybe admire, perhaps all of these potencies at once. But tlaquaches are not like hummingbirds or jaguars. Tlaquaches are opossums. They live under our houses, in dilapidated sheds, in great montes, we find their bodies in, or by, the sides of roads—they eat ticks, they carry their young on their backs, they lay in the hot sun in the middle of a street or road and die and are run over again and again, if no one picks them up. If they are picked up their bodies are frequently trashed. There is no burial, no grief for tlaquaches.

iii.

Behind my heart, or just under it, left in that dry dirt, in the weeds of things I do not like to think about—I am not a good man, I fear. But even not-good men deserve love and want it.

If I say it, will I believe it? If I write it, will you believe me?

iv.

When my husband and I moved in together, he expressed horror over the fact that I knew a tlaquache lived under our house. It is an old house made of wood, with too many rooms, and two fireplaces, one of which is now buried in one of the walls. Since 2008, I'd lived in the house, having left for two years, but returning with my new husband, after my second lover took his life. The house was built in 1925. It is a large house, and true to the time period, it stands atop piers and beams. There is a crawl space, and to access the crawl space, there is a small wooden door on two grey hinges. The door is the size of a large shoebox, maybe one for keeping boots or Stetson hats. Plumbers and electricians have entered the crawl space to perform work underneath the house, and late at night, after walking dogs or upon parking in the driveway, I have seen cats and skunks and tlaquaches using this door. My husband also saw the opossum, one night, pushing its grey body beneath this door, out into the rest of the world. My husband gave it no second thought: he wanted it gone.

v.

The first man I ever loved was not an animal lover. But he loved me, perhaps more than any other human ever has, perhaps more than he loved even himself.

The second man? An animal lover who once, as a boy, rescued a raccoon he called Bandit, and in our time together, also rescued a young blind skunk one dusk, keeping her in one of the bathrooms in our house, and he fed her and cradled her until I convinced him that her best chance lay not with us but with an animal refuge an hour outside of San Antonio. He wept the whole drive home after we dropped her off. He wouldn't let me console him. Indeed, this man loved animals, more, in fact, than he cared for me, or for himself, or for any other human in the world, except perhaps his mother.

When he doesn't know I'm watching, the man I love now is so sweet to our new dog that I think my heart will whistle so loud it will give me away. Four years ago, I never thought I'd see the day. Over Thanksgiving, when we lost our pit bull Kimber, I think he wanted to cry, though I never saw him do it if he did. At its worst, sorrow can destroy a man. At its best, sorrow will show us who we are, who we can be.

As for me, I will always be an animalero. Ever since I was a boy. Dogs, cats, owls and other pajaritos, jaguars and ocelots, wolves, coyotes, and armadillos, of course, and, of course, los tlaquaches. But dogs, especially dogs—I feel most at ease when I am home with my family of dogs—I don't know how else to say this. Perhaps this is my pack, perhaps I, too, simply yearn to belong.

vi.

When you are a boy, you also might have a pack. As part of a pack, you also have the choice to go along with shit or to eschew it. When you are a boy, so often, it is true: the world is yours. When you are a brown boy, the world is and is not yours. A queer boy, too. We are told this in so many, many ways. And so, it is, in fact, routinely easier to go along with racist shit, to laugh at rape jokes, to join in or silently acquiesce as people are ridiculed as faggots or illegals. But these beliefs are not yours. No. None of us owned this shit. Not when we were born, not when our skin first tasted air, not at the moment of our first scream. It was given to us, placed over our bodies like a heavy coat of sticker burrs and tar, forced upon us, even. Eventually, though, we make it ours. We choose. If we don't molt that tar-burr coat given to us by the world, if we don't cut away those patches of shit clinging to our hands and our chests, then, we accept those burrs. Accepting them means we are okay with these violences enacted upon others. And often, and tragically, enacting these violences is a way to say we belong, that we are members of the pack. Yes, we choose the kind of boys, the kinds of men we become. Or if, even, we don't become men at all. At some point in our lives, gradually. All of us. Molting, choosing, tar, chest, power and burrs.

vii.

If I tell you I once believed only good men deserve love, what will I say next? If I tell you this is an old story, a story older than fire and bloodshed, will you believe me?

viii.

Perhaps it is the fact tlaquaches are maligned for their queerness, for that pouch they shouldn't have or use, for their semblance to other dismissed animals like rats, that we carry aversions to them. "They are so fucking ugly," someone told me once. "So gross."

I will not try to explain away others' disgust for these animals as much as I will try to convey the idea that ugliness is a variable, and the truest discoveries in life also live in the realm of generalizations and variables.

Once, years ago, when I first moved to San Antonio, I bought a camera, and one night sitting on my stoop, I watched a tlaquache make its way out of the alley across my caliche driveway in front of my second truck to the landing below the stairs—a small, square, concrete patch, where I threw food for the stray cats who lived around my house. I watched the little animal eat. I watched it move slowly, watchful and weary at first, and then eat more profoundly, swallowing the morsels as if, in fact, the creature knew pleasure and comfort and wanted joy to last. I tried one night to capture the not-so-small tlaquache with my new camera. I waited by the house. The porchlight dim; my camera on a tripod; my little dog asleep inside. Back then, I did not know much about lighting or shutter speeds and apertures, so when I clicked the trigger, the animal froze and then as I tried to adjust the focus again, the noise startled the animal who took off, leaving its meal behind, abandoning its joy, abandoning it for safety—swiftly, he scurried beneath and then behind my truck and back into the overgrown alley.

ix.

When I was 12, I watched my mom's boyfriend and his friends beat the shit out of a opossum with a baseball bat. Maybe I was 13. Maybe I was one of them, maybe I am a lie.

x.

And so, it is an old story. Older perhaps than story itself. The boy and the men. The boy and weapons. The boy on the hunt. The boy and the expectations, the duties he will fill. The boy on the farm, in the field. The boy standing before the great sky, the darkness of trees, the wide expanse of his breath, the one inside him, the one he is putting out into the great world. But the boy who isn't what a boy is supposed to be and be and mean. But the boy who doesn't want blood on his knuckles–not in his teeth, not on his clothes, not on the ideas that make themselves swirl in his head like a clutch of starlings. Not at all. Nothing like that.

xi.

Like a thread. I heard it one night, as I lay in bed, my arm pressed against my husband's chest, my arm harboring the soft pull and tug of his lungs—that reminder that something inside him meant there was something also inside of me that moved, even when my eyes shut, when I forgot I was living and fell deeply or not-so-deeply into my sleep. We lay there, my husband and me, and the dogs lay beside us, the big mastiff by my side of the bed, her snoring wakeful and overblown, and beside my husband, on the other side of the room, the boxer mix we'd rescued a few months before, after our pit bull died unexpectedly one night and the house felt emptier than it had in a very long time. Each night now, my husband and I lie like this, and sometimes, the house is as quiet as a thumb; sometimes, it is quieter, a noiselessness that echoes an impossible silence so near the center of San Antonio, the city where we live. But one night, I heard that thread. In the other room, across the hall, that long thin hair of a noise. The boy boxer stood up, and I could see his thick shadow at the doorway, his ears up and opened, and he looked back at me, asking, *Do you hear that, too?*

Long ago, I feared being the only one awake in the house. I can tell you those reasons, but first I have to explain them to myself.

I think it was the boxer mix, Sweet Baby Ray, the rescue group named him, who first heard the baby tlaquache who'd entered our house. It isn't hard for me to hear the dogs get up in the middle of the night (when I was a child, I listened for people moving around the house, the trailer, the apartment, at night—perhaps you know what that is like, listening for doom, hoping it wasn't coming, but knowing well it could, and would, like it had before, come to you, to others you loved, gripping bedsheets like they were your tongue or the wind inside your bones, all the while knowing this wasn't life but it was yours—and if you know this, then, for that, I am sorry).

And I didn't know, not at first, that it was, in fact, a small tlaquache who'd somehow made his way down the hall, but he found himself in or led himself, maybe (allowing him more volition), into the laundry room, where I used to feed the small hairless dog we called Tiny, back when he was still alive. (Blind and using only his three good legs, Tiny ate separated from the other, bigger dogs, so that he could eat his fill unbothered, and frequently, he ate to his belly's content, leaving only a few morsels of kibble in his bowl or beside it.) I imagine when the baby tlaquache tiptoed his way through our house, he'd caught the scent of Iams, and I say this because I don't know about the capabilities of opossums' sense of scent, so I only imagine, like I only can imagine my heart beating with something like a starling—one of them, separated from the rest of the clutch, as they dance, as they move along, as they leave to some place better than before.

I haven't ever enjoyed being the only one awake in the house, especially not when I was young, but that night with the little tlaquache in the laundry room, I was glad it was only me, as I don't know exactly how my husband would have taken the sight of the little uninvited animal in our house, holding a morsel of kibble in his two tiny paws, eating and eating and just across from our bedroom.

And soon, I could hear it, too. The sound of teeth breaking into a morsel. Sound of chewing. Sound of a sound I didn't want to hear while the whole house stood without light.

It took me no time to jump out of bed, and I found it in the laundry room, behind the grey mop bucket, in a corner, near the bowl where the blind hairless dog we called Tiny took his dinner every night. From the laundry room door, the boy boxer stared at the small animal.

I remember thinking, *James is going to freak.*

I remember Baby Ray looking up at me like, *What should I do, dad? Do I get him? Dad, can I?*

xii.

Each of us decides, a decision already made before us.

"It's the way of the world," a man I met outside a bar told me one night, seeing my sadness, as we drove to his apartment, my hand in his lap, and a doe, dead on the side of the road.

But is it, really? The world's way—or ours?

Isn't life what we make of it? I thought, as his big body lay on top of mine, as his breath gnawed at my chest and he asked me to tell him the story of all my tattoos. Easily, I could whisper those stories, all of them, pushing my rosary and spider webs and the name on my neck deep into his chest hair, into his breath made of Listerine and cigars and loneliness, but I couldn't stop thinking of that deer beside the road. But even with the dead deer on my mind, I let him kiss me, and I couldn't tell you the rest, as I can barely recall it now, all these years after those facts.

It's the way the world works, que no?

The forgetting, the dying, the deciding.

Yes, we decide to do with the world or it does with us. What that decision does inside our bodies, in our soft mouths and our even softer lungs, in the small territories of the soft heart and the crawl space underneath its soft meat?

xiii.

Because all of my life, I have been accused of being a man who is too sensitive. Because perhaps I am too full of the milk of human kindness. Because perhaps I wear it in my beard or underneath it, perhaps on my brown skin, inside my tattoos of eagles and praying hands, of sagrado corazones and other men's names. Because softness is a trait not every man will openly wield. Because there's a price to wearing softness. Because whomever you are, there is a consequence squatting beside your softness, a declaration, a truth, a pillar of lies, a crack made of river water and salt. Because there's a cost to letting your maleness fur with its mottles and its marks, its coat made of cariño and mystery and vulnerability and longing and suffering, joy. Because softness is not muted, and softness screams its name as if the name was bone and dry soil and all the unwanted and wished-dead things moved by wind. Because a body is never just a body. Because softness is the body, but softness is also the breath of holiness inside each of us, which is love of life, which is an awareness that people and things outside of ourselves do matter, which means connectedness, and which, if you are like me, means God.

xiv.

As I flipped on the laundry room light, I worried the boy boxer might go for the creature, having already killed an opossum on our patio one night.

(A small thing, I found her near the steps, her fur damp and matted and slobbery from where my dog had taken her small body into his mouth. So tiny, *like a kitten*, I recall thinking as I picked up her limp figure and set her on a white cotton towel in a box. I remembered the dog's mouth frothy, a foam formed around his muzzle. And I'd like, now, to think he didn't know what he was doing, that in him there isn't a killswitch, a blood-hunger waiting to ignite, some inherent tendency that propelled him to take her small body into his teeth, squeeze down, and shake, but perhaps that absence of instinct is even more terrifying. As much as I say I am an animalero, there is so much about the animals around me I don't know. I suppose on most days I am okay living without touching their secrets. With heaviness in my mouth, I set the little tlaquache's box by a tree in the front yard, and I stepped away, hoping the idea of living was more than an abstraction, that it had more traction than a sigh, more mass than the simplest of all hopes. In the morning, she had stiffened. I'd feared this likelihood like a tree branch, like a gust, like a hole underneath our house, whispered. And while I had hoped really to find an empty box, I walked out into the yard wearing only my sleeping shorts and stoicism. I'd locked the dogs in the house. Whining that they wanted out, the two big dogs watched. And I stood beside the tree, holding my own hands, looking at lifelessness, at consequence, at her.)

With the small tlaquache eating kibble in front of our washing machine, I put the boy dog in the bedroom and shut the door, and this woke my husband, so I told him, "Keep Baby Ray inside. There's something in the house."

I tried first with a wicker basket to corral the small opossum, and I also had a towel to throw over him, an approach I learned from my second lover when he rescued a skunk—if you cover them in darkness, they might not fight you.

But the small opossum, with its small opposable thumbs, quickly made his way out of the braided container, and before I could get the bath towel around him, he rushed down the hall, under a door to one of the spare bedrooms, and under the closet door.

Opening the closet door, trying to grab the baby opossum with the towel, he hissed, and at this point, I had to ask my husband for help. The small guy shit himself in the closet, the fear on his body; I don't know if opossums can see possibilities, potentialities, but I know that he saw me and he saw my bigger hands and my husband standing behind me, holding a flashlight. I don't need to imagine his terror. I can still hear him hissing.

In the end, we used a red plastic bucket, and I walked the little guy outside, as the boy boxer stood at the side door wanting to follow me. I imagine those moments in that bucket—the small opossum may have lived panic and perhaps confusion, a feeling of being trapped. Perhaps, too, he understood danger, clawing against the red sides, sliding down, unable to grab hold of anything that might lead to a way out.

That night, I let him go near a tree in my front yard.

xv.

I've known this for a very long time: Some of us let monsters into our houses. If they come, we let them stay. Sometimes, they knock. They might wear politeness and civility on their faces. Maybe they place themselves in our lives strategically, grooming us, grooming out our distrust, giving themselves good light. Our mothers let them in, our fathers, too. And if your mother or father or grandfather or some other family member is that monster, does that mean God let them in? Eventually, when we begin to see what or who they are, we may try to send them out, but they come back, even if we block entrances with sofas and books, even if we nail shut all the windows and doors, lock them with muscles and prayer, even if we agree not to tell another living soul.

xvi.

Even shame is a weapon when wielded as such. Which proves that anything can be weaponized. Which proves that anything can be carried around in a pouch, taken out. Anything can be made to bleed.

xvii.

But there is another story, too. An old story. Old, too, like that other story. The story of a boy who does it. The boy who doesn't walk away. The boy with blood on his hands. The boys who kills. Knuckles, whole fists, measured-and-unmeasured hands that did what boy-hands and boy-bodies are, indeed, told to do. And, after the fact, he might look back, and he might miss home or know wrongness, because he accepts indifference is an indictment of godlessness. This is an old story, too. And this is a long walk home, the long arms, or the short ones, hanging beside the boy's body, dripping with the abstractions of guilt, of confusion, of new consciousness and shifting, dripping with despair, because it is, indeed, a painful thing to live with one's blood deeds. It is a painful thing to walk away from the boys we are supposed to be. Violence will haunt a boy even when he forgets it's there.

xviii.

And I'm going to tell you another story. This is the story of how I am not good. This is the story of contradictions and walls. A story of bricks and opossum bones. This is the story of failing, which is the story, then, of what kind of man I have become and how. Early in my life, I decided that while I didn't know what type of man I would be, I knew the type of man I would not be: vicious, cruel, spiteful, unaware. I wanted to be kind. I wanted to carry compassion in my hands like a kite. The feathers, the talons, the long-sharp beak and eyes. Really, all my life, I have just wanted to be good. Really, all my life, I have worried that I was not good.

xix.

You see, there was an opossum living under our house several years ago. This bothered my husband, and he wanted him out. To appease my husband, I read about ways to distance a tlaquache from the place he or she calls home, which happened, also, simultaneously, to be our home, the one my husband and I moved into that summer when I told my body it was alright to love him.

I tried sprinkling cayenne pepper around the crawl space door, red powder staining the concrete. I tried running my dogs around the house, after reading online that dogs' scents can dissuade opossums and skunks, although I'd already tried the cayenne pepper, which seemed to only dissuade the dogs. So then I tried dipping rags in dog urine, which seemed implausible at first, given that my dogs piss in the grass and the earth being the earth does what it does, however, by this point Tiny, the small hairless, had begun eschewing the grass for his business, opting instead for the concrete. It was easier, then, to soak rags in puddles of Tiny's dark yellow piss and lay them out by the entrance to the crawl space. But I admit, as much as I wanted each of these tactics to work, as much as I would have taken any of these solutions, each of them flopped. The opossum would not give up his home, or hers, which also was mine and James's.

When I admitted I'd failed, James suggested we block the entrance.

"We can't trap him in there," I said, after a few moments, judging my own words, harnessing them and not wanting the words that the heaviness in my mouth made to grow sharp or fling out like the jaggedness that was happening inside me.

In certain ways, I was dispirited by the idea of making the opossum leave. And while I didn't expect to fully convince my husband of the benefits of keeping a tlaquache around, I did my best to promote the idea that opossums eat ticks and other bugs and even, I've heard, run off rats. There is nothing deliberate, though, about not wanting to force a creature out of its home—and I say this fully aware that it was because, and only because, it was a tlaquache that I felt guilt wad up inside me like a hive, exterminating any rat I would have said *fine* to.

But didn't I say all creatures want love? And deserve it?

But didn't I say I wanted to be a good man? Kind and not cruel, conscious of my hands?

xx.

Then, too, there is the origin of *opossum*. The word comes from the early 17th century—from Virginia Algonquian *opassom*, from *op*, 'white,' and *assom*, 'dog.'

If my grandmother from Coahuila were still alive today, I might ask her what she knew of the word *tlaquache*. She would hold her long braid, the ends of its grayness, and she'd hold out her hand, which was a reminder of what happens to brownness when it's old, and she might tell me what I already know, which is the word itself is brown, browner than me, brown like aguacate like Tenochtitlan brown like xoloitzcuintlis and tierra and time.

So maybe it's the brownness of the animal I love.

So maybe it's the likeness to dogs.

Or maybe it's the story. In other words, maybe it's the guilt I will forever carry when I watched and did nothing as my mom's boyfriend and his friends beat the shit out of an opossum with a baseball bat.

xxi.

Someone, right now, is thinking, *It's just a fucking opossum. Just.* Just.

xxii.

Someone, one time, said, *They're just queers and hookers and junkies.* Just.

xxiii.

At this point in my life, I do think my mother's second husband hated me, because he knew I was queer. Do I need to prove it? Of course not. Not my queerness, not his hatred. What's there to document?

I know he hated people like me.

My mother knew he hated people like me. She told us. I think back then my mother knew I was queer, also.

Back then, I think my mother hated us too.

And so, what becomes of one's body when two truths inside you face off? When two things you know to be true, on a collision course, bare their teeth and glare? Who wins? Who do you help? What side do you pick, if not your own?

My mother was lonely. She was lonely for a man.

Perhaps you know that kind of loneliness. I know that in the middle of my years, I do. And so I can understand, now more than halfway through my own life, that sometimes the body will do what it has to do to not be lonely.

But hurt is hurt, and hurt is one of those elements like a rock standing in a yellowing field or a tree branch that's broken off but hangs, still, unable to fully separate from the rest of the tree: joto. Joto.

Joto, if you can hear the bones breaking in another human's mouth, then, you understand, like I understand, like we understand—there is no need to prove shit. No need to pick up the stone smeared with shit and hold it up to the light so others will believe its truth, there in the lines of your palm. No need to climb the broken tree and point to the hinge, no need to grab the splinters, that juncture where togetherness ended its hold on the tree and the forces at work set in.

It's not that hard to know when people hate us.

And after the fact, what else is there to write down or photograph or sing of except the simplicity of hate. He found me ugly. I reminded him of something or someone from who he was before, and he wanted me gone.

I don't need to tell you my mom's second boyfriend, who later became her husband, ran me off. I was twelve, maybe thirteen. He did it with beatings and insults, by killing that opossum, and by wishing me not there, which is the way men often do.

There are stories I am not going to tell you.

In any case, we begin to learn this tenet early on in life if we are watching: if we see something as ugly or unworthy, as lesser, then it is easy to allow it to be thrown away, to be uprooted and removed, to be smashed with baseball bats and condemnations, whole fists, silences and vitriol, lies and laws, ultimately destroyed.

We begin by watching others do it, hearing it transpire in our houses, on playgrounds, in locker rooms, when no one is looking and also in full plain sight of those who might put a halt to the torture. And one day, one day, we do it ourselves.

xxiv.

I am willing to concede that none of us is as innocent as we'd like to be.

I am willing to concede that I have hurt other things, other people.

I am willing to concede that there is a luxury and privilege to the act of washing blood from our hands.

Yet, I am not willing to concede the pain of this story. In this sense, I am a man. In this sense, we will always be those boys.

xxv.

In the end, I will tell you that one night, after the gym, my husband and I drove up to our house to find the opossum, just leaving the crawl space, illuminated in the driveway by the headlights of our red Ford. The animal scampered, climbing over our small retaining wall, into the neighbors' dark grass.

James did it quickly. In minutes, he'd walked in darkness back behind the wooden shed, emerging with a few bricks, his hands gripping the stone as if stone itself could be both resolution and broken promise. On a night with the summer overwhelming the air, my husband stacked the bricks in front of the crawl space, and I went into the house to tend to the dogs, to give them their food and cariño, to refill their water. In moments, my husband entered the house—he had blocked the entrance.

What's done was done, and we went to bed, after eating, after watching the late news, and in the morning, we made love, and I made breakfast and I kissed him goodbye before going to work. I figured the little tlaquache would have to find another home. It's just the way things worked, in life, in this life I was making.

But the truth is we didn't know that there was another opossum, thinking that only one of them lived under our house. What happened next is a damn spot on my hands, proof that I have stopped begging stars to hide their fires.

Perhaps I am only making excuses for myself, as men often do. Perhaps I am trying to defend what James and I did, or redefine it, as men often do. But there's no way I could have known another opossum was living beneath our house when we shut off the entrance to the crawl space. Admitting that is fine, though it does nothing to alter the fact there are bones trapped somewhere in the walls of our house.

xxvi.

When the exterminator came, it was because the smell of something dead had permeated half the house. The front half: the living room and the office and the kitchen, the hall by the mantle, the fireplace, and one of the bedrooms. The man wore a blue suit, which he put on, over his clothes, to go under the house. As he crawled under my house, I stared at the inside of the crawl space door—there were scratch marks embedded in the wood, snagged on the splinters there was fur. There before me was what I, what we, had done.

After fifteen or so minutes, the man in the blue suit who was supposed to find the dead thing emerged, although he'd found nothing, except a hole underneath the house, he said, near the big fireplace, that led up into one of the walls.

"We can punch out the walls. To find it," he said.

I asked, "How will you find it?"

"We'll just have to start breaking through walls. We could find it the first time. Or we could go through all the walls."

Somewhere a tlaquache had died in our house. I thought of that desperation, of trying to escape a house that wouldn't let you out. When he, or she, died, what was I doing? Was I lying on the floor, playing with my dogs, whispering sweetnesses to them, stroking their long necks or their bellies? Was I reading the book I was rereading at the time, Anne Carson's *Autobiography of Red*, or writing some draft of a shitty poem I was trying to make good? For all I knew, James and I were opening each other up as the small animal took its last breaths, as it suffered and struggled and finally surrendered to death. For all I knew, I was feeling sorry for myself or looking at the parts of my body I don't like in a mirror when it died. I don't know. I don't.

In the end, we did not punch through the walls.

"It will go away after a few days. Three or four of them," the man in the blue suit who'd been under my house said.

As a result, I hung bags of charcoal in all of the rooms. On doorknobs and in closets I hung coal. I found them at Lowe's, near the rat traps and/or the air filters, I can't remember exactly. I sprayed aerosols, but the combination of rot and cinnamon fucked with my head. Even tobacco leaf candles and boiling orange rind did little to quell the air. And for a few days I watched the dogs sniff urgently at the house. The mastiff sometimes pawed at the floor, and I wondered if there were other things living under my house, trying to get out. Every so often, I caught a whiff, and in time, I removed the bricks and let the door again be moved.

xxvii.

But hurt is hurt, and we each carry it around. Some days, we pass it off or around; and too often we aren't even aware that we're pushing our hurt off onto someone, asking or telling and perhaps, tragically, even forcing someone else to carry it.

xxviii.

Splinters and lightning and the echoes of things that, over all of these years, have stuck to our skin and our bones and our hair— alley or monte or room or field, crawl space, or inside the walls of us, maybe a red bucket, maybe a box, maybe a backyard under a streetlamp by a fence, maybe a pouch that has grown inside us. The world is what we make of it, que no?

xxix.

The truth is I was glad when my mother's second husband left her. Or when she left him (even all these years later, I don't know which version of the story is truer). I understand now that to him, like to millions of others, my queerness, our queerness is monstrous and therein must be displaced, interrupted, destroyed.

In Carson's book, Heracles loves the monster Geryon. Or more accurately the other way around—the monster Geryon loves Heracles, who is cruel, who will be the monster's good death, his pain, his one volcanic memory.

I admit there are times in my life when I pursued monsters, when I loved them and thought I could save them. From themselves, from the world, from me.

All creatures want love. I believe that. I will say it. Again and again.

I don't think tlaquaches are monstrous at all. I am enamored with images of mama tlaquaches carrying pups atop their backs, traveling, taking them all. I am enamored with the idea of the pouch they are not supposed to have. Or we.

To someone, right now, I am monstrous for what I just said, for what my husband and I unknowingly and knowingly did to the tlaquache beneath our house. Some days I can be washing dishes or sweeping up the dog hair, and I remember there are tlaquache bones embedded somewhere in our walls, and then, I believe I am monstrous.

To someone, when I hold my husband tonight, when we lay in our bed and I turn off the lights and I press my brownness against his body, that will be especially monstrous. (I hope you and your loved one(s) are partaking in that monstrosity too.)

The pockets of men are monstrous, also, to some. The pockets of women are monstrous to others. The pockets of those of us who are *they*—their pockets, also, especially, now, in these times, are seen as monstrous by some and are under attack.

It's not that hard for others to know when we hate them. It's not that hard to know when we are hated, or when we hate ourselves.

But even monsters can be missed; even the monstrous can be yearned for.

I suppose some days I have to remind myself that all creatures deserve love, deserve affection—including myself, including the parts of me and the memories I don't love.

I suppose sometimes I have to remind myself that all of the world is stark naked, it is, at some point, when no one or when everyone is watching what we do.

House Call

Melissa Lozada-Oliva

katharine is getting her monthly brazilian wax **$$** she isn't seeing anyone **$$** so this isn't for anyone **$$** you shouldn't do anything unless it's for yourself **$$** katharine is a self-made kind of woman **$$** mami is too **$$** katharine comes to the house & mami waxes her in the living room **$$** she makes me set up the dining room table into a waxing bed **$$** the same one we eat our twisted thanksgiving on **$$** arroz con gandules even tho we aren't puerto rican **$$** sweet potato casserole recipe mami got from one of her clients **$$** katharine comes on time **$$** she has no tolerance for people being late **$$** i am reading in the kitchen but eavesdropping **$$** immigrant kids know how to listen **$$** it is how we get ahead **$$** we are good little spies **$$** katharine says have you heard about this george zimmerman thing? **$$** mami says no, what is about? **$$** katharine says well everyone wants to make it a race thing but it isn't a race thing because george zimmerman is *latino* **$$** mami says okay lift up your legs **$$** mami says to be honest, i don't really get it **$$** katharine says i just don't know why people have to be politically correct about it **$$** later, katharine will play devil's advocate with morals on facebook, later still, she will say we are all immigrants, aren't we **$$** now she says i mean you came here & worked so hard i just really admire that **$$** mami calls my name **$$** meleessa please heat up de wax $$ oh, katharine says, your daughter, i haven't seen her in ages **$$** is she still reading? she is so well-behaved **$$** you did such a good job with them **$$** you always do such a good job

yosra strings off my mustache two days after the election in a harvard square bathroom

Melissa Lozada-Oliva

there is very little light in here,
but we're used to this.
we worry about taking too long.
we worry someone knocking
on the door, someone asking us
what we're doing here,
someone making us leave.
before this, yosra jokes
about lining her hijab with safety pins
while we waited for a white family
to clean up their table, the white father
stared at yosra for too long
& said *i'm so sorry*, referring to the crumbs
& coffee stains he & his family had made
they had made this mess not thinking
we would have to sit here in it.
still, at the same time, we tell him,
don't even worry about it, because we have done
all of the worrying for them our entire lives
because we have learned to forgive
every space we enter, because our mothers
have taught us to bring cleaning supplies

because yosra always keeps a roll of string
in her purse for emergencies.
& the emergency, this time
is i'm about to see a white boy & i want him
to like me, my mustache looks like a stock ticker
for money i will never have
or subtitles to a foreign movie
with an actress i will never look like
maybe, one day, i'll actually be chill
like the white girls, the ones who don't shave
for political reasons, the ones who took
an entire election cycle to grow
out a tuft of armpit hair, who say, *you are crazy*
it's all in your head why don't you just love yourself more,
i don't even see it what are you talking about!
the tragedy is everyone was trying to be nice
while denying the emergency that bloomed
around us. yosra sees the hair because she knows
where to look. okay, she says, putting the string
between her teeth, *this is the most middle eastern thing*
i've ever done. & i think of what the most
guatemalan-colombian thing i've ever done
is & maybe it's grow. i think about the most american
thing we've ever done & it's hide in this bathroom.
i think about the most womanly thing
we've ever done & it's live anyway.
this isn't oppression. this is, *i got you.*
i believe you. it hurts but what else are we going to do
it aches but we have no other choice do we.
yosra tells me she's leaving, says, *i'm not going to struggle*
for a country that doesn't even want me.

& i think of the spanish word Ojala,
derived from Arabic. meaning, god willing.
if god wills it. if god wants it.
if i even believe in god anymore.
if Yosra, mercilessly, lovingly, stringing the hairs out
of my face is a kind of prayer, then god will it,
then god damnit. we will live in this low light
i tell yosra *okay, let's go, i'm ready.*
but she says, *no, no. hold still.*
we are not done yet.

Swinging from A Chandelier

Gessy Alvarez

Melissa had something to tell me. We had arrived late at a party in the East Village hosted by some crotchety writer who was making a name for himself after a negative review of his first novel appeared in *The New York Times*. We were surrounded by a group of young, lanky women who were awkwardly dancing in place, beer cans bopping, postures slouching, taking tentative steps like marionettes. Many of them wore short dresses with colorful tights, their shaggy hair falling past their shoulders. Their bangs, long enough to cover their eyebrows and accentuate their eyes. I hunted for something to calm me.

I asked one of the Marionettes for rolling papers, so I could enjoy the stash of bud I found in Crotchety's cookie jar. When I finally scored some banana-flavored *Bambu*, Melissa tapped me on the shoulder.

"Want some?" I said. The taste of synthetic banana numbed my tongue.

"I'm sleepy," she said, yawning into her fist.

"It's not even midnight."

She looked at me, and at the joint I held between my thick fingers. She knew how much I hated to smoke once someone else's saliva slathered my joint.

"Sabi, I have to go soon," she said.

"Is the awkward parade getting to you?"

"I thought we were going to a quieter place."

We hadn't hung out for over two weeks, and I was beginning to feel rejected. After several pleading texts, Melissa finally agreed to go out tonight.

"What's the matter, pretty Melissa?"

"I went to the pharmacy today to pick up something in the lady aisle," she said hiccupping.

I cut her off. "It's absurd, right? In one aisle, diapers and condoms. Lube and tampons. Feminine hygiene products and pregnancy tests. Wait, is something wrong?"

"No. Yes. I'm turning 35, and I'm not married. I mean I don't want to be married…"

"I love that about you," I said.

"No, listen Sabi. I have no one."

"What are you talking about? You have me."

She stood up straight and placed her paw on her belly. She not only bit her nails to the nail bed, she liked to chew through the skin on her thumb, gnawing at hangnails and flesh but never ripping the skin. Her fingers were always pink and tender.

I knew whatever she had to tell me would make our night go down south and fast.

"Wait a minute," I said and waved to Joaquín who walked into the party. I hadn't seen him since that night last month, when I raged at the Film Forum after some idiot decided to stand up in the middle of the leaves scene in Bertolucci's *The Conformist*. I stomped my way down the aisle and demanded he give me back the $15 I spent on my ticket. Joaquín buried his head in his popcorn. He knew, of course; I was lying. I'm a Film Forum member. My ticket was only $9.

Joaquín, being the diehard Bertolucci freak that he is, stayed in his board-thin seat and acted like he didn't know me when the usher rushed in and kicked me out. I ran to the bar on the corner where there was always a line to get in to see the band, but I knew the bouncer. He's a second or third cousin from the Heights who once asked me to write him a paper on the Bronte sisters, and he got an "A," and it was the only "A" he remembers ever getting.

All night, I texted Joaquín, but nothing. And now he's here, and I was about to let him have it. In the three years we've known each other, Joaquín was the only friend I could lure to art openings and film houses. We had the kind of friendship where we could sit at a café for hours reading and not talking to each other. A friendship based on acceptance. He did have a nasty habit of leaving me stranded though.

Melissa, who knows when my mind starts running the marathon, put her hand on top of my head and said, "Calm down."

But I never listen to Melissa. I took off after Joaquín, and he turned, pulled my full-figured body into his long arms, squeezed me, then took a good look at me.

"Ugh, what are you wearing?"

"Is that all you're gonna say to me?"

How could I stay mad at him? It's true. I hadn't thought my outfit through for the shitty party. My hot pink librarian sweater had shed its bright fluff over my black slacks. The pants rode up my crotch, so I kept pulling down my pant legs, but pulling the leg meant stretching the fabric in front of my upper thighs. I had pockets of air there.

Joaquín scowled. "Are you wearing a bra?"

"Yes, you idiot. But I hate feeling constricted, so I get my bras a size too big."

"It defeats the purpose."

"Wouldn't my boobs sag anyways because of gravity and what-not?"

"You need to worship *Anna Wintour*," he said with clinical seriousness.

"Who the fuck is *Anna Why No Tour*?"

"You ARE a lost cause."

"Hey, hey," Melissa said, "why don't you two kiss and makeup."

Joaquín leaned in to kiss my cheek, but I pushed my hand in his way. Without hesitation, he kissed it. Then he walked away to grab something to drink or a hookup, who knows.

I needed to find a spot to smoke the banana joint I hid in my bra.

"Sabi, I really need to talk to you." Melissa would not let it go.

I spotted an open window down the hall. I lunged at it. I wasn't going to let her ruin my night. And more than anyone she would understand. We've been hanging out since we were twenty, enjoying New York City and crashing at friends' apartments. Back in the day, I had to be there for my family. I owed them that. And when I married Nick on my 30th birthday, a church wedding even though we were atheists, I committed to him, but he knew my need to take off, that Melissa was my last go-to escape friend left. Together, we didn't have to pretend to be good girls.

A tall, bearded guy fixed his eyes on Melissa. He came over with two Red Stripes. He handed Melissa one bottle, but she refused. I grabbed it and tried to gulp it down, but my gag reflexes kicked in. I choked and spat more than a mouthful of beer and foam all over Melissa's jeans before she could jump out of the way.

"Really?" she said, looking at me the way she did whenever I switched subjects in the middle of our conversations.

"Oh geez, sorry," I said frantically trying to wipe the beer off her, but she swatted my hand away and walked to the kitchen with the bearded guy chasing after her. I rushed over to the open window relieved to leave everyone out in the living room swaying awkwardly to a remix of Fleetwood Mac's "Tusk."

Alone finally, I panicked because I didn't have anything to light my banana boon with, and then this giant in cargo pants and heavy construction boots came out of the bathroom. I didn't think he even noticed me until he reached into his back pocket and pulled out what looked like a tiny grenade.

I stared at the little black missive in the middle of his massive, calloused hand. When I didn't move, his finger flipped open the top and then pushed a trigger. A small torch appeared. It looked like the engine fire of a fighter jet. I stood still near that tiny jet flame careful not to singe the ends of my fake lashes that I had just bought at the drugstore for $1.99. They took about half an hour to glue on. I surrendered my joint, and he placed it on his dry, wind burnt lips. He lit the joint but didn't take as deep a drag as any good American would.

When he handed it back, I said, "Thanks." His body, a foot and a half taller and wider than everyone in the party. I sucked on that little joint like a vacuum cleaner. For a second, the deep inhalations made my vision go blue.

The Giant barely nodded before lumbering away.

I had two hours to go before running to the Port Authority to catch the last bus to my beautiful suburban neighborhood where my neighbors were either online jacking off to some porn or in bed snoring with the air purifier buzzing on the loudest white-noise setting possible—drowning out the solitary train whistle that breaks the monotony of suburban peace at 4:22 every morning, the bane of every light sleepers' existence.

Nick had grown up in the South Bronx, back when it was called Fort Apache. He didn't want to spend his adult years fearing his neighbors, so to him, the suburbs were a haven. I was devoted to Nick, so long as I could come and go as I pleased.

A remix of Joy Division's "No Love Lost" played in the living room, and it was a guitar slashing, kinetic drum-beat that only those tweaking on Dexedrine could dig. The rest of us, deadheaded types, could only stand with hands on hearts, freaked out by the bouncy vibration playing in sync with our heartbeats, and wondering, how the fuck did the DJ know the beat of my heart? That guy deserved the

Nobel Prize for figuring that out without any scientific training.

The Giant stood in the kitchen drinking a tallboy, talking down to the crotchety writer like he was a kid lost in the supermarket. Crotchety stared up at the Giant with a big fake smile on his face. He waved at the awkward Marionettes, no doubt hoping they would come over and flirt with the Giant, but not one paid him any mind.

I said, "Right on, sisters!" as I shoved them out of my way. I headed towards the Giant and Crotchety who now looked at me with the most dazzling smile on his cherubic face. I smacked his sweaty cheek playfully, took a sip of the Giant's tallboy, and asked him very sweetly, "Is there something I can help with?"

"You've got to tell these people the party's over," the Giant said to Crotchety.

"I bet ya if you gave the music a chance, you'll get into it, and what's wrong with staying a little longer and getting a free buzz on?" I said.

"I just came off a fourteen-hour shift," the Giant said.

"Doing what?"

"Construction."

Crotchety pulled on the neck of his Justin Bieber t-shirt.

"If you're lucky, a boy will pinch your nipple." I attempted a sexy Mae West wink, which I then followed up with an unintentional horselaugh. The Giant wasn't convinced.

"Come'n. You need a drink," I grabbed the Giant's hand and tried to drag him, but he didn't budge. Joaquín was still in the living room smoking a royal blue Fantasia cigarette.

"Whoa, girly, I'm not sure you're my type," he said as he tried to pull away.

"Don't be fussy. I'm married. Five years."

"Where's your ring?"

I dropped his hand and pulled out the ring hanging from the

gold chain around my neck. "My fingers are like sausages, and today I'm retaining water because Aunt Flo is about to hit the town like a tornado."

"Jesus, what's with you?"

"Sabi!" I heard Melissa's voice. She was standing behind me.

"What already?" I looked into her bespectacled eyes.

"I'm pregnant."

"Congrats," The Giant said. He shook her small, chewed up hand with his two massive ones.

"Rich works in construction."

"That's all you are going to say to me? I'm pregnant. PRE-GOS."

But we had a silent pact. She was my fun friend. The free friend with no interest in family or marriage. No man or woman was going to be responsible for her happiness. She had me, and she had her colleagues and students. That was supposed to be enough.

"Are you keeping it?" The protective way she held her body away from me was enough of an answer. Shit, the baby will be real.

"Let's go somewhere quiet to talk."

"I can't leave Rich here alone with these wackadoos."

The Giant turned his attention to the dying party. Crotchety picked up the beer bottles strewn around the kitchen. Out in the living room, Joaquín was putting on his leather jacket.

"Wait up, Joaquín! I've got time for one more drink." I yelled across the living room.

"Boiler Room!" Joaquín answered as he walked out the door. He wasn't going to abandon me today.

"Oh yes, cheap cocktails. Divine," I said because the last time we had ended up at that bar, one drunk guy had called me Rita Hayworth, and I know I don't look anything like Rita. But, on a good hair day, I make an ugly Rita, and Ugly Rita is much better than what I look like on my bad hair days.

"You're a piece of work," Melissa said. "Call me when you're ready to talk."

I watched her walk away, her paw still on her belly as she shoved a few chubby boys out of her way. She couldn't have been too far along. She was still petite, but there was a tension in her shoulders, and the usual sway in her hips was gone. Her body gave off that you-better-step-off vibe that we had mastered at hip-hop shows back in the day when we'd be surrounded by boys wanting to grope any girl that walked in their way.

"How can she do this to me," I said more to myself than to the Giant, who just stood by me staring.

His dark eyes softened. Maybe he understood what it was like to have no one? The table lamps around the room made everything look golden and warm.

Just then Sia sang, "I'm gonna swing from the chandelier," and I remembered that one time that I was on a health kick and pushing through the elliptical machine at like 2.5 mph and that song came on. And my legs pumped that machine so fast that, for a moment, I flew. My body tingled. My heartbeat jumped to 161 bpm.

The party crowd was leaving; Melissa wa probably halfway to her Queens-bound subway; and the Giant's dark eyes were on me. He waited for me to—I don't know—rip my hot pink sweater off, wipe away the moisture now forming in my eyes and under my nostrils. *Fly like a bird through the night; I won't look down, won't open my eyes.*

Poe Park

Li Yun Alvarado

Bronx, NY (1847-Present)

From this cottage,
where he heard
his young cousin-
bride, Virginia

(our Annabel Lee), fight
her own lungs to draw
one last clean country breath,
you can hear screaming

children wrestling
under red and green
monkey bars, or the murmur
of The Ortiz Funeral Home
waiting across the street.

Blood Out

Lizz Huerta

You never forget the day the gifts show up.

The day my blood first came I lay belly flat on Jenny's scratchy bedspread, watching *Saved By the Bell* and wondering if Mario Lopez was prettier than me. He had dimples. I didn't.

At the commercial break I went to the bathroom Jenny and her big sister Mandy shared. The sticky brown paste on the crotch of my panties looked nothing like blood and smelled like raisins. I didn't recognize it for what it was. I thought maybe I'd had a tiny bit of unwiped poop that had wandered from butt to crotch when I'd squeezed my thighs together imagining Jesse and A.C. doing it. I wiped at it with toilet paper and went back to flop on Jenny's bed. Mandy darkened the doorway, holding up a brown paper grocery bag.

"I got what you need, do we have a deal?" She came in, snatching up the remote, changing the channel to MTV. Axl and a supermodel were having a picnic in a graveyard, then sinking together underwater. Mandy sang along. Jenny grabbed the bag and peered inside.

"You're *the best sister ever*." She rummaged through the sack, grinning, "Thank you, *best sister ever*, for staying in tonight to watch movies with us." Jenny winked.

"Whatever, shithead. I cover for you, you cover for me," Mandy winked back. They did a weird choreographed handshake thing. I clenched. I wanted a sister. I wanted a television and candy apple-scented body wash. I got Jenny instead, the closest thing to a friend I'd known. It wasn't hard to be friends with her, all I had to do was listen and nod.

I didn't bother lying to Mom, it wouldn't have worked anyway. We had no secret handshakes, no winks. We had honesty. Mostly. I'd started omitting things, interjecting what I thought were contemplative silences into our conversations. I didn't tell her how uncomfortable life was on me then, how at almost thirteen I was rattling around and at the same time constricted in my body and thoughts, lonely in a way I couldn't articulate.

"Chel, my heart?" Mom knew it was me as soon as she picked up. I thought all moms were like that.

"Hi Mom, we're going to Crystal's tonight, then coming back here to sleep." I picked at the sticker on the wall phone, the puffy kind, smiling cotton candy that had been scratched and sniffed into bareness.

"Ah, and who's staying with her?" Crystal's mom was gone. A week earlier, Crystal had woken up to her aunt burning bacon and smoking cigarettes in the kitchen. Crys was used to her mom disappearing and didn't ask any questions; she ate her burned bacon and stole makeup out of her aunt's purse.

"Her aunt, still." I accidentally peeled the cotton candy face away, revealing a cloud shaped piece of foam.

Mom was silent. I stayed quiet too. Her silence was full, it grabbed at me. I closed my eyes and fought it. She sighed.

"Call me if you need anything Chels, anything. Promise?" She had her Voice on. I promised, we said our I love yous and hung up. I tried to ignore the buzzing around me. I wouldn't call, I told myself. I wouldn't. I rolled up the sticker and stuck it behind the phone, wedging it against the wall.

We rang Crystal's doorbell. The sun had just set, kids screamed and rode their bikes around the apartment complex parking lot. She lived in La Hacienda. Crappy apartments that were stuccoed mission-white and planted with aloe, agave, and sage in an attempt to recreate someone's nostalgic idea of Old California. We'd all carved our names into the nopal paddles.

Crystal's Aunt Trish opened the door.

"Girls!" She said a little too brightly, squinting at us. I didn't know it then but I'd meet dozens of women like her in my life, their skin just a touch too loose over muscle.

"Thanks for letting us coming over," Jenny grinned, thrusting the bag at Aunt Trish, "We bring gifts."

"Giiiiiiiiirls," Aunt Trish cried, pulling a six-pack of wine coolers out of the bag, a pack of Virgina Slims 100s nestled between the bottles. She shook her head, letting us in, "You're terrible, how did you even get these?"

"Aunt Trish," Jenny used her super good-girl voice, "It's the last Friday before school starts. You deserve to relax too."

"I'm not giving you any," Aunt Trish said, twisting open a bottle, "No way, Peach is my favorite."

"They're all for you," Jenny said, "Though we might bum a smoke or two." Aunt Trish took a swig, winking at Jenny and called "Crystal, your girlfriends are here!"

Crystal emerged from the one bedroom. She and her mom shared it except for the nights Crys would wake up to a man carrying her into the living room to deposit her on the sofa. She saw me and glared.

"Her? For real?" Crystal gave Jenny a look, turning back into the room. Jenny followed. I could hear their voices and felt cold all over my body. Crystal sometimes hated me, sometimes hated Jenny. I never could figure out why. I didn't hate either of them, I just didn't want to sit alone at lunch. I let them ping-pong me back and forth, the loose end of what I wanted to be a triangle. I went to the small kitchen and sat on a stool at the counter.

"There's something else in the bag." I picked it up and shook out the CD she hadn't noticed.

"*Rumours!*" Aunt Trish held the Fleetwood Mac to her chest, "I fucking love this album. How did you know?"

I shrugged. I didn't know how I'd known. I'd seen the CD on the wire rack in Mandy and Jenny's living room. Something about the cover, the tiny white woman in a dance pose and a wispy cape, reminded me of Aunt Trish. Not physically, Aunt Trish dyed her hair blue black, but there was something about her, a graceful ache that made me feel like she belonged in a different world.

"We're going to get rolled tacos and ice cream," Crystal announced from the bedroom doorway. Jenny looked past her, not at me and I knew I wouldn't be going. "Jenny and I have something to talk about, we're going alone."

I nodded, spine rolling forward. I crossed my arms over the sunken feeling behind my bellybutton.

"That's perfect," Aunt Trish smiled wide, there was a space at edge of her smile where she was missing a tooth, "I wanted a little time alone with your friend Michelle."

"Ixchel," Jenny said. Crystal rolled her eyes.

"I don't eat dairy anyway," I said and regretted it when Crys and Jenny exchanged a look.

It said *See?*

When the aluminum door slammed behind them Aunt Trish opened two more wine coolers and held one out to me. I hesitated.

"Have a drink, and fuck those cunts," she tapped the Slims against her hand shook out a couple of smokes, offering one to me. I shook my head but took the wine cooler. It fizzed on my tongue, sweet sweet, it tasted like the smell of air fresheners my dad sold in his muffler shop. Aunt Trish opened the sliding door and sank into the sofa. I sat on the other end, taking tiny sips.

"Put in the CD, Shelly," she said. I did. As soon as the first guitar strums started Aunt Trish leaned back, closing her eyes, rocking her head. She smiled something a little sad that seemed to settle on her, like she was covered in dust. I blinked a few times but it stayed. I put my wine cooler on the stained coffee table and picked up a magazine.

I was on tip 27 out of 50, *Put an ice cube up your you-know-what when he goes down on you! The chills you'll feel will have NOTHING to do with the ice!* when Aunt Trish sighed and lit her third cigarette. She opened her eyes, staring at me. I felt her, even with my eyes on the glossy page.

"Is your mom really psychic?" I looked at her. Her eyes were bright and small. I wondered what she'd heard. Mom wasn't *psychic-psychic*, not like the 1-900 number ladies, not someone who read the stars like Walter Mercado, but she was something. She said I was something too, I just didn't know it yet. I shifted and looked back at the page, Aunt Trish laughed.

"You don't say much, Shelley? Let my asshole niece and that spoiled shit boss you around. You're too fucking nice, don't ever be a nice girl. Don't." She ambled up from the sofa and sway-danced to the fridge to grab two more wine coolers. The gloss of her sadness darkened into something else. My palms itched. I wondered when Crystal and Jenny would be back.

"I don't have a lot of friends," I said, looking at the door, wishing I wasn't alone with Aunt Trish.

"Me either, 'specially not girlfriends," she chugged half a wine cooler and held the other out to me. I pointed at the one on the coffee table, still full. "Those two would've finished that and more," Aunt Trish collapsed onto the sofa, closer to me this time. "But you're better than them, smarter." She closed her eyes again.

I puckered my mouth, the sweet taste of peach in my mouth soured into something tasting almost rotten. I went to the kitchen to get a glass of water. Aunt Trish was singing along, her voice too high: "*And I wish you all the love in the world...But most of all, I wish it for myself ...And the songbirds keep singing like—Bullshit!*"

There was a smash, glass breaking. At the sink, I jumped, feeling a rush of wetness between my legs. I grabbed my crotch with one hand, pressing my palm against the strange feel of liquid in my panties and stared out into the living room.

Aunt Trish had smashed the wine cooler bottle on the coffee table. She held her hands, fisted against her eyes. Blood and tears ran down her face and neck. She was still singing along, her voice rough. The carpet glittered with broken glass. I grabbed the roll of paper towels, went to her and held them out.

"You're bleeding," I said. She dropped her fists and stared at me, I saw the web between her thumb and index finger was sliced open.

"*You're* fucking bleeding," she laughed, a scary laugh, "Jesus fuck, Shelly."

I looked down. The crotch of my white imitation-Bongo shorts was red, bright red. I stared. I wanted to cry. I wanted my mom. My hands began to shake, aching, I opened and closed them. I took the paper towels and ran to the bathroom. There was so much blood. I didn't know there would be so much blood. I sat on the toilet, gasping as something fell out of my body. I looked in-between my legs into the basin. A chunk of something, almost black, wisps of blood snaking away from it. I wanted my mom. I wiped as much of the blood as I could. I opened the bathroom cabinet but there was nothing there but cotton balls. I accordion-folded toilet paper, lining the crotch of my panties. I opened the door.

Aunt Trish hadn't moved. Blood ran down her arm and elbow. The shadows around her were darker. The only light shone from the kitchen. She smoked a cigarette, staring up at the popcorn ceiling.

"This your first blood?" She asked, exhaling a cloud of shapes. She squinted at me, I nodded. "Wanna celebrate?" She shook the pack of smokes at me. I shook my head. I wanted to leave but the blood on her was begging me for something, somehow. I felt the sadness pouring out, thick; it smelled like the bathroom at a gas station in the desert, like disappointment.

I grabbed a sweatshirt, tying it around my waist so the arms hung down in front, covering my bloom of blood. I ran down the stairs. The kids had been called in for the night. A few men sat in the back of a pick-up, drinking beers, a ranchera playing from the open window of the cab. I saw what I wanted, what was calling me.

I knelt in front of the plant the way Mom taught me. I touched the stems, closed my eyes and asked permission. Waited. I pulled one hair out of my head and wrapped it around one of the leaves as offering, then snapped another off, the mucous of it trailing. I ran back upstairs.

"Aloe vera," I held the spine of plant out to Aunt Trish. Her eyes were unclear, red. I used my thumbnail to slice the aloe open, cracked it and went to her. I took her hand, the cut one, and wiped the clear innards of the plant over and over her wound. I hummed a little, something else Mami did when she did the things other mothers didn't. *Heal, heal, little frog butt.* I closed my eyes, her hand limp in mine.

Summer. A weathered man, fingers like sandstone. One hastily packed bag. A kiss on sleeping sister's face. Desert gas station bathroom. Blood in the panties. Not period blood, hurting blood, breaking blood. Hot vinyl of backseat cracking against bare thighs. The grapevines heavy with summer, jumping a fence with him to gobble mouthfuls. He was kind, mostly. Miles upon miles. Motor inns. The men nearly better than home. Nowhere far away enough. The guilt of leaving, Trying to make it up all these years—

I snapped my hand away, the aloe flying across the room, I stepped backward, the glass crunching beneath my canvas tennis shoes.

Aunt Trish cracked her eyes open.

"Jesus fuck, what are you?" She whispered and was asleep the next moment.

I tried to pick up the glass. The carpet was too thick. I couldn't find a vacuum. I didn't want to be there anymore. I grabbed the bathroom rug and threw it over where the glass was. I felt the toilet in my panties bunching, slipping. The CD finished. I sat on the opposite side of the sofa from Aunt Trish, the blood soaked tissue creasing against me.

I heard steps in the concrete stairs. One set of feet, two, three? I wondered who Jenny and Crys had found.

"What happened to Aunt Trish?" Crys stood in the doorway, kicking off her flip-flops. She had mint chip spilled down her front. Jenny slid in behind her, her fake-good smile plastered. I shrugged. The third pair of feet were home. My home.

"Mami," I swallowed, standing up. I still had the sweatshirt tied around my waist.

"Why'd you call your mom?" Cry asked, her black eyeliner was too thick, smudged.

"I didn't," I said.

"Liar," Crys mouthed at me.

"I needed Ixchel, so I came for her," Mami passed both of them, she was wearing one of her long, wide scarves, red and violet. She pulled it off and playfully tossed it to me. I took it, wrapping it around my waist like a skirt, dropping the sweatshirt on the couch.

Aunt Trish sat up, blinking. She looked around, at me, Mami, Crys and Jenny.

"Party," she said, but her heart wasn't in it.

"I'm taking my girl home, thank you for being a part of this," Mami said. She leaned down and wrapped her arms around a surprised Aunt Trish. I knew those hugs. More than arms and skin, she was Giving. She kissed Aunt Trish on the side of the face, whispering something to her. Aunt Trish stiffened then went slack. When Mom pulled away from her, the dust I had noticed earlier was dissolving, leaving Aunt Trish clearer. I blinked.

"Why is the bathroom rug on the floor in here. Why are you so weird?" Crys said, picking up the wine cooler I'd never finished, going for a swig. Aunt Trish reached over and snatched the bottle away from Crystal.

"Wash your face, right fucking now," Aunt Trish snapped, she turned to Jenny, "And you, just, fucking stop being such a shit." Jenny gaped, then followed Crys to the bathroom.

Mami tilted her head toward the door, I didn't say goodbye. I hurried out, down the stairs. A marine layer had moved in, cooling the night air. I looked for Mami's car.

"I walked," she said. She pulled a plastic grocery bag out of her pocket and handed it to me, "For your shorts and panties." I ducked behind a car and pulled everything off, bunching it up, wrapping the bag tightly several times over.

We walked. We didn't talk. I walked with my knees close together, scared the blood would fall out of me, spill onto the sidewalk. Mami led us through the park, humming. Leaving the sidewalk, she kicked off her shoes and walked in the grass. I followed. She knelt in front of one of the peppertrees. No grass grew underneath it (the peppercorns that fell were too acidic, something in my memory told me). I knelt beside her, the dirt soft on my knees after I brushed away a few peppercorns, keeping my thighs clenched. Mami put her hand on my lower back, I unclenched.

The first few drops ran down my thighs, itchy, thicker than water or pee. Mami rubbed my lower back and I relaxed more, let my hips drop a little. I heard the plops, blood hitting dirt, another clot passed out of me, hot and wet.

"Let it out," Mami whispered, "Let out what you took into your body."

A carousel of images whirled by. *The desert gas station bathroom. The taste of sun-warmed grapes. A baby who looked like Crys, snot running down her chin, diaper-less, standing at a window, crying. Faces. Too many faces.*

Another clot fell from my body, I gasped and opened my eyes then closed them again. *Mandy and Jenny huddled in one bed, blanket over their heads as crashes and screams rang out. Mandy singing to Jenny to drown out the—*

"Into the earth, Ixchel," Mami whispered, "Out of the earth. Use your hands."

A hot rush of wet. *My father's apartment the weekends I wasn't there. Staring at his own hands, how the grease and oil framed his nails, darkened the callouses.*

I pressed my hands to the earth. There were no more faces. The smells of mud, water, decay. Below that I felt something flowing, not water, not air, something that rang in my veins. Roots, tendrils, fungal spores waiting on the right conditions, all speaking to each other.

"I called you, Mami," I said.

"I know." She said.

Drawing Maps With Sandra Cisneros

Sandra Cisneros

Also in attendance: Angie Cruz, Clarissa A. León, Armando García, Adriana E. Ramírez, Elizabeth Rodriguez Fielder, Tanya Shirazi and Angela Velez

We began our conversation drawing our own personal maps of the United States. We had met for dinner in downtown Pittsburgh. Drawing jump-started our conversation about latinidad, place, writing, privilege, power, and activism. We discovered how some of us were able to map all of the states, including Mexico, the Caribbean and Central America, and others could only remember the places we have traveled to. In the end we journeyed together in conversation remembering and thinking through how we work and continue to work as Latina/o creatives and scholars.

Angie Cruz: One of the reasons we started *Aster(ix)* was in response to the question, who is publishing women writers of color? Through my work with the journal I've realized how many writers of color, even the more established writers, are having a difficult time placing their work, especially when the work is not performing their identity politics. But also we have found that women of color don't always submit their work. They need to be solicited.

Sandra Cisneros: I don't send my poems out unless someone asks me.

AC: Me neither, and this is true for many women writers I know. So then people are like, what happened to her? Is she publishing? That's one of the reasons we started *Aster(ix)*. To find each other. To put our works in conversation with each other.

SC: We had a women of color journal and it created a place for Cherrie Moraga, Ana Castillo, me, and others: Third Women Press. It published us. It didn't get support from the university because Norma Alarcon didn't want it to be controlled by them. But that's how we found each other. And it's really important.

AC: I was really inspired by that conversation we had many years ago, when we spent a day together in Torino. You said one of your inspirations to found Macondo was your commitment to push writers to make their very best work.

SC: The reason I also created it was because I thought that we needed those networks. So many of the Macondistas continue to edit each other and connect. They don't feel necessarily that they have to keep supporting Macondo because they have their own community. But there's younger people coming up. It needs to continue. We still need that network, that zócalo where to meet.

AC: A lot of writers that I know, especially those that are sending their work out, feel if their work doesn't legibly appear to be Latino/a—it has a more difficult time getting placed. What do you think?

Adriana E. Ramírez: I think it's less so in nonfiction.

AC: But what Latino/a in nonfiction that is published isn't writing about a Latin-American/ latino/a problem?

AER: It depends on who you are. If a Latino/a historian is writing about the history of the Apache, I don't think that's necessarily performing your identity. I think it's a unique perspective of a historical thing. I can't divorce myself from who I am. I look in the mirror and see the nopal and everything. You are who you are. Even the way I use language, the aphorisms that pop up. Even "Cero a la izquierda," doesn't even sound right in English. "Zeros to the left"?

AC: I do think the dearth of Latina writers getting published each year makes creating spaces such as Macondo and *Aster(ix)* an urgent matter, even if neither of our activist efforts are by no means exclusively Latino/a. What I also realized is how many writers, because they are activists, mothers, etc., don't have the time and space to write. I think we desperately need writing residencies, where we're asked to do nothing but our creative work.

SC: But don't you think too that some part of not making the time to write is also that we make ourselves too available? Regarding activism, I think when we rescue, it's because we're rescuing some part of ourselves too. That's what a therapist would tell you. You're rescuing, but you're rescuing yourself too. Where you don't feel you do enough, or you feel guilty because of your success or whatever it is. That's why I started the foundation. I felt guilty there wasn't more success for others.

AC: But, Sandra, if you hadn't started Macondo, who was going to do it?

SC: I also did it because unless I invited them, I couldn't get the writers I wanted to see to come to San Antonio. I needed my oxygen supply and my water supply.

AC: But you also changed so many people's lives because of Macondo. Like VONA Voices, and Cave Canem. Like Toi Derricotte who put a lot of energy into Cave Canem. If she wouldn't have done it, who would've done it? So there's always that thought too. Not that we should be doing this work forever.

SC: Oh, I think we should do it, and then we should pass the baton. You don't have to do it your whole life or you don't have to do it for ten years. I think you can do it for as long as you can do it and once it had a good run somebody else can start something else. I often wonder if we make ourselves too available as women. We have to stop. I did two foundations, and I gave fifty fold. I don't have to feel like I'm a bad person now.

AC: Do any of you feel a pressure to be activists or give back? If so how?

Tanya Shirazi: I worked in educational outreach for eleven years before I finally decided to fully invest in my creative writing pursuit. I went to grad school in counseling. It was hard to leave those altruistic career spaces—I made close connections with first-generation Latinx undergrads. They are my second family. When I decided to pursue an MFA and leave I felt selfish. In my heart though, I knew it was time to nurture the creative part of me that I had ignored for so long. Sometimes we have to find a balance in how much we give to other people as well as to our craft.

SC: When Ursula K. Leguin turned 60, she went into sanctuary. She calls it sanctuary. She says *I can't. I'm in sanctuary.* And that's what you've got to say, 'I'm in sanctuary.' When I come out of sanctuary, you can approach me, but don't tell them when you're coming out of sanctuary. Never come out of sanctuary. You know, just go into sanctuary and say,

'Not now, I'm in sanctuary.'

AC: I love it. That's what I'm going to call it, my sanctuary. It's like what I used to tell my family when I moved back into my old neighborhood to get out of family commitments; I would say, 'Estoy estudiando.' 'Oh! Estudiando, esta bien!' 'Estudiando' was like the magical word. If I was studying, everyone left me alone.

SC: Yeah, que bueno to have that kind privacy.

Angela Velez: In my house, the only door that locked was the bathroom door.

AC: Yeah, me too. I grew up that way. No privacy.

AV: No one bothered me there — I would just run the bath tub for 30 minutes and lock myself in and read my book. It was the only privacy I could have.

SC: A lot of houses don't have doors.

AV: And I shared a room anyway, so a door is a privilege.

SC: When I was in middle school we moved to a house where I had the only bedroom with a door in the whole house but I couldn't close the door because I had a big piece of furniture. The room was really tiny, like only a twin bed could fit in it and a dresser and a little corridor this wide - to get to the bed and open the door. But the furniture was longer than the room and the door couldn't close because of the furniture. I had a door, but I couldn't close it. It had to stay open like this much.

*

AC: So, I have a question. Some of my writer friends have told me I have to go into 'sanctuary' so I can finish my books. They say I am doing too much. So it makes me wonder what do you think is the role of the writer? The responsibility to her community?

SC: You do what you can and then you have to pass the baton on to the people you helped.

AC: So, it should be cyclical.

SC: Yes, yes. You already did your work. You say, I helped you, now you got to pay it back.

AC: What do you think about the new generation of writers?

SC: I don't know the new generation. Who do you mean?

AC: Like, the younger writers. What do you think?

SC: I don't know. I don't know them. I mean, I can't make generalizations. I just know I like the work that I see coming up. I only know the books that come to my attention, the Macondistas or the people in the Southwest. No sé. You tell me.

AC: Well, do you feel that technology has shifted community building, do you think it's strengthened it?

SC: I'm very technologically backwards, so I don't know.

AC: But you're active on Instagram.

SC: That's only because my friend Macarena got me to do it. I like taking pictures so it works really well for me. I can't even type with two thumbs. I type with one index finger. My friends said that we're going to start evolving and having smaller and smaller thumbs.

*

AC: Sandra, you've always been so good at creating community. When you were in San Antonio didn't you meet with other writers and approach them to write together?

SC: When I was in Chicago we would meet in my house, and we would have workshop, and we would meet in cafés like this and just buy a coffee and a croissant and pass manuscripts and write together. We weren't writing, we were editing. And when I got to San Antonio, and I could afford to donate a workshop week, I started workshop at first at the Guadalupe and then it was in my kitchen table and then it just kind of grew from that

AC: You don't share your work anymore?

SC: I do share my work. Like my friend, Ruth Behar, edits my essays. Did you know she's got a new young adult novel. A first novel.

AV: What's it called?

SC: *Lucky Broken Girl.*

AV: There are a lot of young Latino writers who are young adult authors.

It's really exciting.

SC: It took Ruth sixty years to become a novelist—she always wanted to be a novelist, but she was an anthropologist, and here she was a MacArthur winner, and she was very unhappy because she wanted to be a creative writer and so now she has her first novel and she's 60. I'm really happy for her.

AV: I worked as a young adult editor for a few years. I worked for a packaging company, so we came up with concepts for books, and we contracted writers to write them. It was called Paper Lantern Lit and they sold books to a number of different publishing houses.

SC: And who were some of your writers?

AV: Probably the biggest book is Rhoda Belleza's book. It's a soap opera set in space, and it's very good But for many of the books I worked on, the focus was on creating high-concept, commercial books, rather than literary fiction.

SC: Well, why can't you write literary young adult fiction?

AV: Oh, I think you can, but it's a challenge with a quick turnaround. The literary part takes time and it has to come from the author, and often that's lost in the rush to publish.

SC: A book I like is called *Blood Line* by Joe Jimenez. He's a poet and he did this novel about a young teenager in high school, you know the one who's always getting kicked out of class for fighting, and his mother isn't even his mother. His grandmother raises him and it begins with the grandmother having to invite her son who's like a no-good-bum guy to come back to the house to try and straighten him out and it's just a beautiful, beautiful book. Beautifully written. I don't know how long it took him but I think when poets do that crossover from poetry to fiction, they do great jobs.

AC: Who publishes him?

SC: Small presses. I think there's a lot of good writing coming out of the southwest. Writers that I know from Texas personally. I think the writers that do get published by the larger publishing houses, it's because they are palatable to a white audience.

AV: I think there can be many goals for something literary.

SC: I think publishers need to give young people the best. Because a young person may not read another book again. The difference between a good book and a great one is just time. Don't you think? And I think some writing needs another pasadita, another bit of editing. I think a lot of times writers, especially of color...is it Dr. Johnson who said, women writing, it's not that they write well but that they could write at all. Like a dog walking on its hind legs. Not that it walks well, but that it could walk at all. And I think sometimes editors treat Latino writers not that we can write well, but that we can write at all. And we should not lower ourselves to do work that isn't better than good and that's because people expect us to fail. I've always felt like people expect women and people of color to fail. So we got to do better than that.

AC: Do you feel that's true in writing workshops and publishing?

SC: I just feel like we always have to be better than good. You know women have to be better than the guys, and people of color have to be better than mainstream lit. I feel like we got to always be excellent and that difference between good and excellent is time. But a lot of our writers before they came to Macondo were treated with kid gloves in their workshops. Just because they were a person of color. But I like Macondo because you have other people that are your peers that are telling you, this is good. But why can't you make it great? I know that some of our Macondo writers had to take jobs and do books for hire. But I just think if they had a little more time, and if they could come up with their own concepts then they would do it.

AC: I do agree lots of works could use more time, but as an editor sometimes I get a story and give the writer feedback, and they will ignore my feedback, and publish it somewhere—and they are satisfied with just getting it published. And I say, why did they throw away that story? They've already spent a year on it, why not another week? So we are bombarded in general with such mediocrity. To me, publishing mediocre work is another form of pollution. Content pollution.

SC: They're not honoring their work.

AC: They could have given it another few months and try to take it to the next level, and it would have been better for their career in general.

SC: This is the thing that young writers don't realize. I'm on the panels giving them awards. I'm on those panels with the other judges that are looking at that manuscript and if you don't do a good job with that book it's going to hold you back from getting your next book, or getting an award.So every time you put a book out there that isn't your best, you're advertising that you're not the best. So, what do you want, the money? Or do you want to tell people you're a half-assed writer? Because that's what you're advertising.

AC: Right, because as a judge you need to be able to defend the work.

SC: So that's the part that the young people don't get. Every book should be your very best like it's your last book and the only book you're going to write in your life and every book should be better than your last one. Because you're on a trajectory and if you don't do that, that may be your last book.

AC: But also some writers never take the chance to put their work out. I find that sometimes I hold back, a kind of self censorship, or a thinking of an expectation of what I was supposed to be writing versus what I wanted to write. I always struggle with that. I guess it's because I'm one of the very few Dominicanas who has been published in English. But also I wasn't honoring how much I'd changed, and how much I'd grown from the books I had written. I have to trick myself to forget the audience and just write the book.

SC: I think you got to keep the audience out and when you're thinking about the audience is when you're either doing the small writing, the writing where you get your agenda out of the way. You have to work so hard to get your agenda out of the way.

AC: And I see so many writers of color that we solicit for *Aster(ix)* send us work, and I feel this tension in the work, where they are representing culture but also translating their experience to some general unknown audience that almost feels derivative of writing that they've read, or they think women of color should be writing. Writers—why are you writing about this? Is this really what you want to write about? But it's almost like, because that's all they've seen in the context of Latino/a narratives, they're stuck there. When I did research for *Let It Rain Coffee,* I was going to the archive in Santo Domingo to look at old newspapers and the archivist there said, don't make the same mistake that Vargas Llosa did with *Feast of the Goat*. And I said, What do you mean? "He wrote with his head. That's not our people!" He said that Llosa's book was very well researched but you can't feel anything. His advice: write from your heart.

SC: Yeah, yeah. That's the challenge. Edit with your head, but write from your heart., I used to tell people, turn this off, turn this on. When you write, write from here. (Taps chest) And then turn this off and turn this on.

AC: Who was it that said, *write drunk, edit sober.*

SC: Well, I don't think you should write drunk, because it all sounds good when you're drunk—but I think you should write sober and edit sober. That is what I would say, and you don't do them at the same time. Well, I think that when you drink, you're trying to numb yourself. And when you write, it's like driving, you have to be as lucid as possible. Also, writing takes up so much energy. You have to sleep. I can't do it at the end of the day like when I was young.

AC: Last year, I invited Helena Maria Viramontes to do a reading with Mary Gaitskill. Did you know they were born in the same year, came out with their firsts books around the mid 80s? Both of their books were about sexuality and taboo and relationships. I had never thought of them in conversation with each other, but once they were here together, it was interesting to see how different their trajectories were. Gaitskill's book was a literary sensation, framed as a new feminist voice that was changing the literary landscape, and Viramontes' book, when I looked at the reviews, they were all modeling some kind of sociological study of the Chicano community. It was very marginalized in comparison to the way Gaitskill blew up the literary scene. In the end, the trajectory of Helena and Mary—so different. Very different doors opened for each of them. But also while Viramontes was visiting Pittsburgh, I invited Toi Derricotte to dinner and in our conversation, Viramontes shared how her early influences were African American writers. This is also true for me—I was influenced by the slave narratives, contemporary black writers, etc, like Morrison, Baldwin, etc. And I realized just how many Latina writers I know are influenced by African American literature. So out of curiosity I have made it a point to ask non Latino/a writers what Latino/a writers do they read? They often can't name Latino/a writers writing in English. Latin American writers yes, in translation. Unless of course it's Junot Díaz or you. Does anyone have any thoughts on this?

Elizabeth Rodriguez Fielder: It's definitely not compatible with the history of activism between the two groups—between Black and Latinx groups. There has always been a history of activism. Not that it doesn't have its problems. There's always been this shared intensive struggle. I think that it really has a lot to do with academic disciplines that everything gets brought into if you're bringing some things into the university space they have departments that are in different floors and different places.

SC: I grew up in Chicago, a very multicultural city. I was influenced by immigrant writers, working-class writers. I hate to use the word *minority,* because we are the majority in the world. I was influenced by writers of color. I was influence by all of the above. I'm still influenced by writers that are somehow off the beaten path. I was very influenced by the Latino boom. I never like reading who's on the bestseller list. I'm kind of a snob like that. If everyone likes it I don't like it. You know how they do those little surveys? Those little pies? I'm always the 4%.

What I need isn't going to be on the bestseller list. I was looking for somebody more new and obscure. I'm still off the beaten path as far as writers I like.

AC: I'm not saying this as a critique to any writer, but there is some writing that crosses over that is written to Middle America and then there is Latino/a writing that is having a more internal conversation. I think of Toni Morrison when she was an editor and she was interested in writers who were...not like Ralph Ellison. She was like, "invisible to whom?" She was interested in Toni Cade Bambara and Gayl Jones. She was interested in these writers that were writing to her. I think that there's a lot of writers in the Southwest that are writing to each other and not to those folks in the white Middle America.

ERF: I think that's a large aspect of minority literature in Black literature, Latino literature: That there's a difference between writing to the white audience and writing to one's own community.

SC: I think we shouldn't say color, we should say class. That's very important. I identify a lot with some white writers that are working class and not always with writers of color that aren't working class. That's an important distinction.

AER: There's no phrase that I love more than "The U.S. has a class problem that it calls a race problem and Latin America has a race problem that it calls a class problem." I think there's a danger in oppression Olympics—who's had it worse. Like, should Black readers be reading Latino writers, who is owed what? I am very wary of taking two groups that are oppressed and in some way rhetorically pitting them against each other.

AC: But there is an invisibility that comes with the system.

AER: I agree. I would say two things. One, I think it is interesting the amount of Latinos who are killed by police that aren't reported on, and aren't reported the same way. You can see the Black community has mobilized and there's a lot more of a core identity. I think the problem is that we assume that there's a pan-Latino identity and I don't think there is. As somebody who is Mexican and Colombian, it's a different identity than when I'm talking to someone who is Puerto Rican. Certainly, there's also a class divide. El español que yo tengo es un español que definitivamente marca mi educación, y de dónde soy, y el acento lo dice. The fact that I don't have an accent in English either, speaks to certain privilege. It's tough to negotiate all that. Second, I want to ask you Sandra—Do you think your writing is palatable?

SC: I don't know, I'm not a white person.

AC: Your writing is read in a certain way, but if you read it closely it's really subversive and radical in a way that it's not palatable if people read it with all the subtext.

SC: There's a lot of subtext and I always tell the kids when I visit schools and talk to them about *House* [*on Mango Street*]. I tell them you know more than your teacher about this book. You are the authority. Why is that bike for sale that the girls buy? Why does Tito have to get rid of it so fast? And they know that's a hot bike. It's stolen. But it's not in the text. The kids know. A lot of little things like that, they aren't spelled out for someone unless you're from the barrio or a community like *The House on Mango Street*. I always tell the kids, you know more than the teacher.

AC: I'm curious for those of you who represent a younger generation of writers, up and coming, what does the literary landscape look like to you?

AV: I think it's a little different for me. I'm really interested in writing young adult literature. There's a strong push right now for diverse books. There are visible leaders that are putting pressure on editors. People are supportive and asking for new kinds of narratives. That feels very exciting. I've seen my friends get books published and their books do really well, and they are writers of color and who are being read cross-culturally. But looking at the adult world of fiction, that looks scary and intimidating.

TS: This is my first year in the MFA program, it's my first semester. For one of my classes, I wanted to write a paper on what is is to be considered an "Authentic American." To me, it's the angle that children of immigrants have to reconcile constantly with others. In their writing, in their personal lives, with themselves. Like Angie said, sometimes I do feel we are forgotten and feel pressured to perform my identity. I wonder how my writing will be received. Where is it going to go under? The concept of ethnic literature is always an interesting one to me. It feels limiting. You can be born here but it still feels like you have to "cross-over." Cross-over from where? The in-between? The borderlands? I feel very much American because I was born here. At the same time, I am very much Latina. I speak Spanish, I am very attached to my culture. To hear someone even question my identity, that I'm not really an American, is still jarring.

SC: You need to remind these people that you were here before the world was round. That's what I like to say about Latinos. We're from the Americas. We have been here millennia before even Europe discovered us. You need to say that.

TS: Strangers have asked me, "Where are you really from?" I respond, "I'm from Los Angeles." But then they still ask, "No, but where are you really from?" My first response isn't good enough. It's not good enough to say that you're not from Pennsylvania, but from California. When they press the question further, I hear, 'You don't look like us, you have to be from somewhere else."

AER: I'm a naturalized citizen. But I've been in the U.S. since I was three months old. So, am I American?

SC: [singing to the tune of 'Natural Woman'] You make me feel like a naturalized American!

AER: I got a little flag and everything. It was great. I was twelve. I had to take a test to be here. I had to wait in lines, do paperwork, I had to be an "Alien" for a really long time. I had a card that said "Alien" on it. Resident Alien. But, I've been in the U.S. since I was three months old.

Clarissa León: How interesting would that be now— with DACA and all that's happening.

AER: The thing is that my parents came here privileged. We came over with papers. My father purchased half of a U.S. business that employed five Americans which is an automatic reason to be granted a visa and then residency. It is not your typical immigration story. But, fun story— I was at PEN—at a PEN-America party. I was talking to some agent and she was asking "what's your immigration story?" I told her roughly my immigration story, and she's like "Oh, so you're not an immigrant, immigrant?"

AV: Someone said something like that to me. I was telling them about Williamsburg, Virginia, which my parents are obsessed with because they like learning about American history (it's new to them). Someone was like, "Oh, so your parents aren't like typical immigrants that came to this country with nothing." What is nothing? My mom was a secretary, and my dad didn't speak English. It was such a weird question to be asked. It was somebody that volunteered for the Obama campaign, was a lawyer, lived in San Francisco.

AER: Ah. Well-intentioned white people.

AV: Yes, I didn't know how to react. What do you even say to that?

ERF: It feels like we have this rich, amazing body of narratives in literature and in our personal lives. And yet, at times it feels as if people can only pick from five stereotypes and categorize everything into them.

AER: It's hard to be a white savior if the people you want to save are ok.

AC: There's nothing to save!

ERF: It's just hard.

Armando García: The question—"where are you really from?"—is common. It's not necessarily unique to any one of us. It happens to all of us. At the same time, I think that if we start internalizing that question as both the beginning and the end of our narratives, then we start thinking about our narratives vis-a-vis that question. Doing so automatically discards the possibilities of what your narrative could be on your own terms and not on the terms of what and whom you're addressing when you respond to this question. Rather than thinking of your work through, "why is my story always being questioned on whether or not it's American?," rather than privileging that question, could you privilege a different one, "What is my narrative?" Period.

ERF: Letting your narrative create new questions.

AG: Right. I don't work in narrative or literature per se. I work in theatre and performance studies. I am in conversation with people whose narratives, which are sometimes written, are meant to be embodied and performed live. Those Latina/o playwrights aren't published in the same way that fiction, poets, or nonfiction writers are published. Theatre's primary mode of circulation is not the printed page. I am also in conversation with young undocumented artists, a lot of whom are writers. For them, the narrative of writing to America and of wanting to be American is problematic if this does not question what "America" and American citizenship mean. Who gets to embody these ideals? Taking the naturalization test, or answering the questions "are you really American?" and "what kind of immigrant are you?" These aren't the beginning or the end. It's not that they shouldn't be engaged. It is that they cannot be the primary focus of our work or of our art. But I am not on or from the outside. I understand that I'm very privileged: I am a U.S. citizen, I was educated at three different Ivy League universities, and I am a professor who has held not one but two tenure track jobs. I understand the privileges that my birth certificate and education have earned me. Nevertheless, while listening to this conversation, I don't know if we should be privileging the American question without questioning why we do so. One of the things that has been happening in Latina/o theatre across the country is this organization called The Latino Theatre Commons. When I attended one of their conventions in 2015, I kept hearing their motto that "Latino theatre is the new

American theatre." But this motto does not in and of itself imply, let alone include, a critical engagement with what it means to be American. Appealing to "America" to include Latinidad does not automatically gesture toward understanding America and its citizenship protocols more critically. This appeal achieves the opposite: it becomes part of an assimilation agenda. The motto is asking to have a piece of the cake too because we too are American in the same way that "you" are American. That you is whiteness because it signifies catering to a white imaginary of what American means... I think that a lot of what I am saying is coming out of my own angst about wanting to find these stories that do not privilege (white) cultural nationalist ideas of America as the beginning and the end of our work and of our forms of art.

SC: Are you a playwright?

AG: I am not a playwright. I used to not even identify as a writer. Helena Maria Viramontes knocked sense into me one day when I told her that I wasn't a writer. She turned to me and asked: "What are you? What do you do? Don't you write?" I said "yes, ma'am, yes." When Helena speaks, I listen. That is when I started rethinking my relationship to writing. Am I a writer? Yes, in a sense. I write academic essays, I've written nonfiction work, poetry, translations, and conversations with artists. I am a writer, in a broad sense. At the same time, I am also a pseudo-visual artist. That puts me in this kind of conversation.

ERF: Even as academic writers, we share a lot of the same pains and processes as creative writers. Things like time, and finding space for writing.

AG: The first time I read Sandra Cisneros was in my Spanish class in college.

SC: Even though my work is in English, you read it in Spanish?

AG: The first time I read any writers of color was during my first year of college, when I took two literature courses. One was called Chicano Pop Culture and the other was called The Mexican Revolution Through Film and Literature. We read "Eyes of Zapata" in the Spanish class because it was about the Mexican Revolution. We read it right after we read Nellie Campobello's *Cartucho*. I think you and Campobello were included in the part of the syllabus that talked about women and the Revolution. The professor included the "Eyes of Zapata" from *Woman Hollering Creek* in that section, and that was my introduction to Chicana literature.

SC: I thank your teacher because that was the most difficult story in that collection.

AC: After your work with Macondo and all these years that you've been an activist, what is something you would like to see as a writer, a woman of color?

SC: I gave Macondo fifteen years. Macondo is old enough to clean it's own room. I started that and I still believe in Macondo and I hope they will find their home and go somewhere. But for me, right now, I feel like I am in a different phase in my life, where I have to focus in the short amount of time that I have left on the planet to grow. I want to grow. I feel like I was just born when I moved to Mexico. I'm in this new phase where I am going to grow spiritually. I think writing is a spiritual act. I don't mean it in a religious sense, I mean it's a spiritual act in that we do work of transformation. We do work of great transformation that heals people and heals our own wounds. That's what I see. The times couldn't be worse. If I'm going to work transformation in such a dark hour, I need to recharge, focus and grow and learn to be wiser than I've ever been in my life. That's what I'm focused on. What's being asked of me keeps getting bigger and bigger. I just don't feel like I have the answers. I don't feel like I have the wisdom or the talent or the vision. I want to be that. I'm working on that: growing spiritually. I have next to my bedside people that I admire— James Baldwin and Gandhi, writers like that. I'm reading on a spiritual level because I'm on a spiritual journey. It's my time to read books that are going to transform me so I can do the best work because estamos tan fregados. We are in the worst time ever. I still want to do the work that's organizing but I need to focus on my own writing right now.

*

AC: Now that you have passed on the baton with Macondo. What is happening?

SC: Macondo still exists but now it's in transition and leaving Guadalupe. They're looking for a new home. I don't know if it'll be within an institution. I like the idea of a writers' workshop for activism. Any color. Any activism. But people who are really serving some community. I also think it's time for them to move. I don't know if they are staying in San Antonio. I would like them to go to another place.

AC: In the southwest?

SC: Not necessarily

AC: What about Pittsburgh?

SC: If Pittsburgh would give them a home, wherever they could get to.

AER: My house!

SC: Macondo is looking for a home. I had to step back so they would step up. I'm watching them but I can't hold them up anymore. Otherwise they won't step up.

ERF: As someone who studies the civil rights movement, I really appreciate the focus on activism. Many of the activists I research never had time to really process and write down or publish their ideas and thoughts because things moved so quickly. So much of the burden of representing the civil rights movement as it was happening falls on the writing of Alice Walker and Toni Cade Bambara. It's a beautiful idea to have a space for activists to take the time to write down what their process has been for them.

CL: Everything that's been said has been very insightful. It makes me think about the stories being covered in the news media and also who's actually getting attention as far as book reviews. I do believe looking at the VIDA count that the Latinx community is getting blindsided from major book reviewers, like *The New York Times*.

SC: *The New York Times* pisses me off. Before we were at least in the back of the bus, but now we're not even on the bus .

AC: I was reading how even though Latino/as make up 25% of movie ticket buyers, we make up about 6% of all speaking roles in film - even if we are 18% of the U.S. population.

AER: It's also us. We are not a galvanized community. We don't work together. There's no Latinx Twitter the way there's Black Twitter

AV: There's a little one.

AER: It doesn't have the same cultural impact. You look at the media that is rising right now, you've got *Very Smart Brothas*, *Black Nerd Problems*, *Awkward Black Girl*. You've got a whole black critical arts community.

AV: There's *Remezcla* and *Mitu*.

CL: But it's also about a representation of the writers themselves. I find it so saddening. The VIDA Count looks at the authors writing across all media in the major publications like *The Atlantic*, *The New York Times*, *Harper's*, etc. I rarely find any Latinx writers there, in some cases there's not a single Latinx writer at any of the publications.

ERF: It's sad that our culture is determined by a small select group of people controlling the publishing industry.

AER: I'm going to be stubborn and say it's us. I'm going to say it's us. Angie Thomas' book is at the top of the YA charts. It's unapologetically black. And the black community has supported it, has bought it, has moved around it. You look at Tyler Perry movies or the rise of Spike Lee. People that are supported by their community, and that translated to ticket sales. We don't support our people the same way because we don't have a solid agenda or cultural identity.

AC: But the Latino/a identity is very complicated with disparate histories and interests.

ERF: And they also support media from Latin America as well. That's the main media house. Like Univisión.

AER: Univisión is the closest thing we have to our unifying force. Jorge Ramos will save us.

CL: I think it's a cyclical thing, representation. You don't see yourself, you're not going to go because you don't see yourself, and it's because nobody is there to make sure there's something for you. I cannot think of a single major motion picture that has a protagonist who is Latinx where she isn't misrepresented in some shape or form.

AC: Or she's not playing Italian, or Greek, or ambiguously ethnic.

AER: *Fools Rush In*, maybe. Salma Hayek

AC: That's so old!

SC: Did you see that movie *Beatriz at Dinner*?

AER: It made me uncomfortable in all the right ways.

CL: *Hamilton*! That's about a white man in American history.

SC: That had to be about a white man or else otherwise white audience wouldn't go see it.

AER: Also, some Latinos identify as white. There is no pan-Latino identity in the same way. We don't have the same cultural backdrop like Black Americans do. A common shared history. Even people at this table. We're all different kinds of mutts.

SC: I like that this conversation began with us drawing the United States.

Laritza

Ivan Velez

MY NAME IS LARITZA FULANO, AND I DON'T LIKE TO EAT SHIT.
BUT THERE I WAS, MUNCHING IT LIKE IT WAS CHEETOS.
COMPLIMENTS OF THE BLESSED SISTER SANGANA PENDEJA DE LA ESTUPIDA AND HER SELF RIGHTEOUS BLAH BLAH BLAH
IT WAS ENOUGH TO DRIVE ANYBODY KOOKOO FOR COCOA PUFFS.
OKAY. I GET THE POINT!
CUT THE SHIT ALREADY!
WHAT?
YOU AIN'T DEAF! YOU HEARD WHAT I SAID. I DON'T HAVE MY BOOK REPORT!
BIG FUCKING DEAL!
IF YOU WANNA KILL ME FOR IT, THEN GO AND GET A GUN! OTHERWISE--
--JUST SHUT THE FUCK UP.
SHIT.
SO I GOT SENT TO SEE MR. WERT, WHO REALLY HAS IT IN FOR ME JUST 'CAUSE I PUT A LITTLE SUGAR IN HIS GAS TANK A COUPLE OF TIMES BUT NEVER GOT OFFICIALLY CAUGHT. I HAD TO THINK FAST.
OF COURSE, IT DIDN'T HELP THAT HIS SECRETARY HATED MY GUTS.
YOU AGAIN. TCH TCH TCH.
BITCH.
SITTING NEXT TO ME WAS MISSY PISSY BAGGY EYES, WHO PROBABLY GOT SENT DOWN FOR SLEEPING IN CLASS AGAIN. SHE WAS ALWAYS DOING THAT SHIT.
AND SHE NEVER HAD TWO WORDS TO SAY TO ANY-ONE.
IN A WAY, YOU HAD TO RESPECT THAT.
1

BUT, OF COURSE, JUST AS I WAS THINKING THAT MAYBE MISSY PISSY WASN'T SO BAD AFTER ALL...
--THAT BOOGER COMES CRAWLING OUT HER NOSE.
SO I TURNED MY BACK ON HER.
HMPH.
?
MISSY PISSY BAGGY SAGGY BOOGER WOOGER YUCK.
BESIDES. I HAD TO PREPARE FOR MY PERFORMANCE
ALRIGHT, YOUNG LADY. I'M READY FOR YOU NOW.
KEEP THE EYES BIG AND WATERY. MAKE HIM THINK YOU'RE SCARED.
SO... YOU REALLY THINK YOU CAN SPEW FILTH AT A DEDICATED TEACHER AND WALK AWAY CLEAN?
NO, LITTLE GIRL. YOU HAVE GONE TOO FAR THIS TIME.
SIT STILL. SHAKE THE HANDS LIKE YOU'RE NERVOUS.
OKAY. KNEES TOGETHER. WATER YOUR EYES A LITTLE. DROOL A LITTLE...
I'M CALLING YOUR GRANDMOTHER. THERE MIGHT EVEN BE SUSPENSION INVOLVED.
NOW GO FOR THE KILL.
I KNOW. I KNOW. I'VE BEEN SO TERRIBLE! IT'S JUST...
MY FIRST PERIOD CAME TODAY... OUTA NOWHERE...
AND... AND... I JUST--
--SNAPPED!
OH GOD WHY DID I DO IT WHY?! SISTER TERESA IS A SAINT! A SAINT! SHE ONLY WANTS TO HELP ME LEARN!
HOW COULD I DO THIS TO HER!
HOW?! OH GOD! WHY!?
OH!
OH!
OH!
I THINK I JUST GOT A CRAMP.
2

A QUICK TRIP TO THE NURSE'S OFFICE AND THAT WAS THAT.
I EVEN GOT TO SKIP HISTORY AND TAKE A NAP.

I WAS THE TEEN QUEEN AND I KNEW IT.
AND SHE--

-WAS MY TOTAL OPPOSITE.

HAH! MISSY PISSY BAGGY EYES!
HAW HAW HAW
GOT YOUR PAMPERS ON TODAY?
I SMELL SOMETHING FUNNY AND IT'S NOT THE LUNCH!

HEY!
AIEEK!
SPLOOT!

HEY! WHAT THE HELL ARE Y-- YOU..UH.. OH-OKAY.
THIS SCHOOL IS FULL OF STUPID ASSHOLE JERKS.

STUPID ASSHOLE JERKS THAT KNOW NOT TO FUCK WITH ME.

WELL, MOST OF THEM KNOW.
AW, JEEZ.
3

SO MISSY PISSY SAT DOWN NEXT TO ME.
AND I LET HER.
AND SHE'S BEEN LIKE MY PUPPY DOG EVER SINCE.
LUCKY ME.
SHE EVEN FOUND OUT I LIVE, LIKE, DOWN HER BLOCK.
I WAS DOOMED TO BE BORED.
AND DESTINED TO HAVE MY GOOD NAME SOILED LIKE HER UNDERWEAR.
BUT THAT'S NOT THE POINT! OKAY, MAYBE IT IS. JUST A LITTLE.
I MEAN, LOOK AT HER! SHE'S A MESS!
HER HAIR'S STRINGY! SHE HAS NO STYLE WHATSOEVER.
AND TO TELL THE TRUTH SHE DOES SMELL A LITTLE TANGY.
SO HOW COME I STARTED NOT TO MIND SO MUCH?
WHY DID I GET SO PROTECTIVE OF HER?
MAYBE BECAUSE, UNDERNEATH THOSE BAGS AND THAT SPLOTCHY SKIN AND THAT MIASMA...
I COULD SMELL A SECRET.
AND NOT SOMETHING TACKY OR DEPRESSING AND AWFUL LIKE BEING MOLESTED OR HAVING TWELVE TOES--
..BUT SOMETHING DAMN JUICY AND AMAZING.
AND, HONEY, THAT WAS A SECRET I HAD TO KNOW.
AND WISH I NEVER FOUND OUT.
4

OKAY, SO WE FAST FORWARD AHEAD ABOUT TWO MONTHS.
DON'T COMPLAIN. I ONLY GOT NINE PAGES TO TELL THIS THING AND THAT WAS ONE MORE THAN I'M SUPPOSED TO.

MISSY PISSY, OR RATHER MELISSA, WAS STILL ACTING LIKE MY SHADOW SHE'S EVEN GOT US MATCHING FRIENDSHIP BRACELETS.
CHEESY OR WHAT?

AND I WAS GETTING A LITTLE BORED WITH IT ALL.
WANNA GET SOME ICE CREAM AFTER SCHOOL?
NO.
HOW ABOUT SOME BURGERS?
NO.
HOW ABOUT SOME PIZZA?
NO.

AND YOU KNOW WHAT HAPPENS TO NERDY LONERS WHO FINALLY FIND A SUCKER WHO'LL TOLERATE THEM?
THEY DON'T EVER SHUT THE FUCK UP!

SHE WAS PARTICULARLY CHATTY TODAY BECAUSE IT WAS HER BIRTHDAY AND I PROMISED TO STAY AT HER HOUSE FOR A SLUMBER PARTY.

JUST ME AND HER.
OH JOY.
AND I KNOW THE IDIOTS WERE TALKING ABOUT US.. SAYING WE WERE CO-MUNCHING AS IF. IN THEIR DREAMS.

SHIT. IF I WAS GONNA GO MUFFY IT WOULD BE FOR SOMEONE MORE FABULOUS THAN MISSY PISSY BAGGY EYES.
WANNA GO TO THE COMIC BOOK STORE?
NO.
WANNA PLAY VIDEOS?
NO.

BUT WHAT IF SHE DID TRY SOMETHING TONIGHT?
WANNA GO SEE SOME OLD XENA SHOWS?
OH MY GAWD I GOTTA GET OUTA THIS!

UNFORTUNATELY MY ALCOHOLIC GRANDMA HAD OTHER PLANS.
WHATCHOO LOOKIN AT? DON' GIMME DAT LOOK!
BUT 'BUELA, I GOT CRAMPS!
SO WHAT? CRAMPS ARE GOOD FOR JOO. MEANS JOO A WOOMAN!
PLANS THAT INCLUDED ME BEING OUT OF THE HOUSE SO SHE COULD GET GOD KNOWS WHAT FROM GOD KNOWS WHO.
YUCK.
5

BUT, 'BUELA! I FEEL SIC--
OKAY. OKAY. GOO' NIGHT! HAVE A GOO' TIME!
SHE COULDN'T WAIT FOR ME TO GET OUT!
BRRR!
DOUBLE BRRR!
DRATS. FOILED AGAIN.
MISSY'S FAMILY WAS AS SAD AND CREEPY AND BAGGY-EYED AS SHE WAS...
BUT THEY WERE ALSO JUST AS NICE, IN THAT ANNOYING NEEDY KIND OF WAY.
AND AS SAD LITTLE MISSY BLEW THE CANDLES--
--ON HER SAD LITTLE CAKE, I COULDN'T HELP BUT SMILE--
--AND HOPE HER SECRET WISH COMES TRUE.
CORNY, HUH?
AND HEY, IF SHE WANTED, SHE COULDA TOUCHED MY TITTY. AFTER ALL, IT WAS HER BIRTHDAY.
BUT NO FINGERPOPS!
BUT SHE DIDN'T. WE WERE ASLEEP BEFORE 'CHEERS'.
I DIDN'T EVEN FEEL WHEN HER FOLKS PUT US TO BED.
I WAS SLEEPING SOUNDLY
WELL, AS SOUNDLY AS I COULD IN A STRANGE HOUSE
WHICH WASN'T SOUND ENOUGH

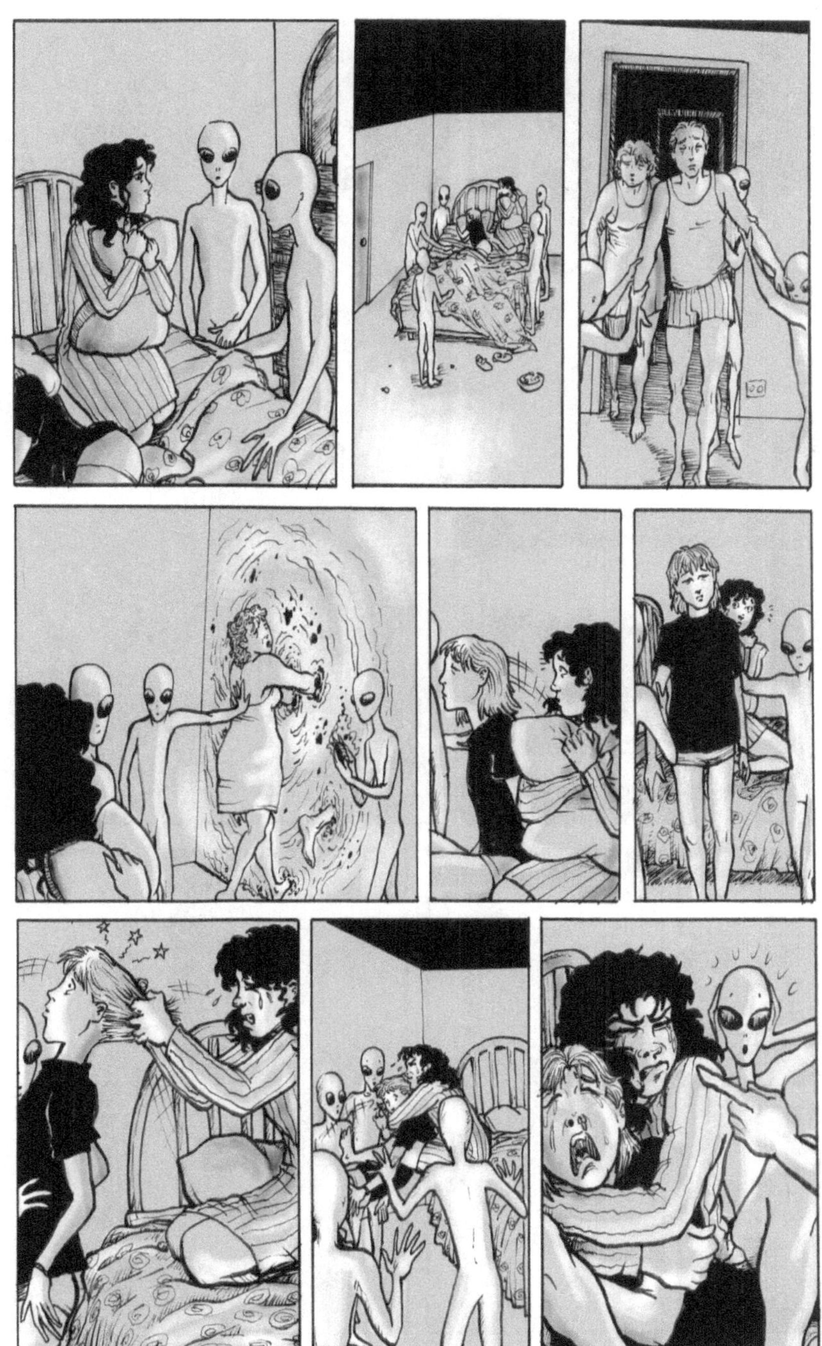

8

WE NEVER TALKED ABOUT WHAT HAPPENED. AFTER A WHILE IT ALL SEEMED LIKE A BAD DREAM.
BLAH BLAH BLAH
A BAD DREAM WE ALL HAD AT THE SAME TIME
MISSY AND HER PARENTS MOVED AWAY ABOUT A MONTH LATER. I DON'T BLAME THEM.
AT LEAST I FOUND OUT WHY MISSY HAD THOSE BAGS UNDER HER EYES.
AS FOR ME, I'M FINE.
I'M ALWAYS FINE
IT TAKES MORE THAN BUGHEADS TO MAKE ME FEEL LIKE SHIT.
BESIDES... THEY NEVER BOTHERED ME AGAIN. GUESS THEY DIDN'T HAVE TIME TO TAG ME.
EXIT
POOR MISSY.
I STILL THINK ABOUT HER AND HOPE SHE'S OKAY
EVEN THOUGH SHE PROBABLY ISN'T.
SHE WAS A HUGE PAIN IN THE ASS BUT KINDA COOL TOO.
FROM WHAT I HEAR, ONCE THE CREEPS TAG YOU, YOU'RE TAGGED FOR LIFE.
BUT THEN AGAIN, WHO ISN'T.
CATM
MISSY AND HER FOLKS GOT TAGGED AND THERE'S PROBABLY NOTHING THEY CAN DO ABOUT IT.
BUT AT LEAST I KNOW, IN SOME SMALL WAY...
...I TAGGED ONE OF THEM BACK.
CATM
LARITZA VERSUS THE SPACE ALIENS
by Ivan Velez Jr. 11/97

The Algorithm Falters

Laura Winther Galaviz

The boy on Match says he wants a girl like Proverbs 31:10.

I haul a Rubbermaid from the basement and find the Bible from my Catechism days, sealed inside since seventh grade, resting on a nest of handwritten notes passed between classes. I pull back the cover, to figure out what the boy is after. He wants a girl who's *up before dawn preparing breakfast.* A girl who will *face tomorrow with a smile.* In his carefully curated exhibit of photos, he curls a dumbbell in front a dirty gym mirror without looking up, falsely unaware of being captured. In the photo's southwest corner is the reflection of a teenage girl holding the camera, the explosion on the flash catching the mirror. Her own dumbbell is waiting at her feet, reps interrupted for this vanity project. The boy on Match wants to know what you can do for him.

In middle school, as a gift to my mother, I offered up two years' worth of Wednesday afternoons to the basement of a church. It's a miracle that only once did I get into a fight with the Catechism teacher. *Marriage*, he told us, *has nothing to do with love*. He insisted, *you find someone that you can make a stable life with and you sign the contract.* Outside of church, the world was feeding us Cinderella and Snow White, Jane Eyre and Clarissa Dalloway, and somewhere in there, I'd come across Rosa Parks and Joan of Arc, and I wondered about the contracts they'd signed, the terms. Why would anyone sign such a thing?

Beauty but humility but sexiness but purity but perfection but humanity but independence but subservience. A single pat of butter spread over ten pieces of toast.

The boy on Match wants to pick out a woman the way I have shopped for shelter dogs. Does it bite? Good around kids? Can it be taught to stay? To beg? I tell the shelter worker, *I am gone a lot. I do not want something that's too much trouble, just someone to sit on my lap now and again*. She tells me, *then you don't really want a dog*. She's right. The boy on *Match* wants to squeeze you into his life between a 9am haircut and a midday meeting.

The boy on Match *loves family*. He has a mother and wraps a stiff arm around her in one picture, eyes straight at the camera, bleached smile a mile wide. She's facing the day with an apprehensive smile. He seems to notice her in the way you notice the seat on which you sit, only when it slips out from under you. The boy wants you to work out. *I am always working to make myself better, you should be too.*

He'll settle when he's found a girl like Titus 2:4—*self-controlled and pure*—is what the boy on Match says. Like a decorative plate, pulled from the cabinet and polished only to be put back in its place—pretty and inanimate—the boy on Match wants your perfect, untouched ass on his arm.

The boy on Match wants a woman fully-formed, delivered by drone.

The boy on Match does not mention anything about the man he wants to be. He sips brightly colored drinks, somewhere warm, with other boys who look like they might be on Match. Who all have tans and gel and board shorts with the same bright blooming flowers. Biceps curled jokingly (but seriously) in every photo. Boys who can never find a *good woman.*

The boy on Match doesn't ask what you want, but we are getting more accustomed to this, to speaking even when we aren't invited to, because we so rarely are.

I want a man like Ellison, pg. 1, *a man of substance, of flesh and bone, fiber and liquids—and I might even be said to possess a mind. I am invisible, understand, simply because people refuse to see me.* Awake and aware enough to be angry.

I'm waiting to be paired with Darcy in Austen:214, *In vain have I struggled. It will not do. My feelings will not be repressed. You must allow me to tell you how ardently I admire and love you*, someone who isn't afraid of the infuriating complexity of loving a woman who owns herself.

I'll settle on a man like Salinger: 256, *God, I wish you could have been there*, a heartbreakingly broken Holden, moved to tears by Phoebe spinning on the Central Park carousel in the wet gray of February. I go there, to the carousel, on an afternoon in April when I am also feeling broken, watch the kids careen, and connect with a complex emotion I've struggled to communicate.

What I want
Ultimately, I guess
is a man who is better read
Who has cracked the spine of more than one book

For my part, I'll promise to be Whitman, constantly contradicting myself, but good-naturedly. How could you do anything else with the multitudes within you.

The algorithm has failed; I'm not the woman you're after. I'm the wrong dimensions—all three, instead of the two you ordered. I don't lie flat, I'm hard to wrap. You would forever be cutting yourself on my edges and piercing my soft spots.

I have an occasional habit of waking at 3 AM, eyes open and brain alight, and turning from side to back to other side, rolling onto my stomach, pillow clenched between arms, trying to find sleep again. The men I've loved have put a hand on my side then. They've asked what's on my mind, and out comes a stream of lyrics and trivia, an article I read earlier, the time in third grade I said the thing I shouldn't have said, the oven that might still be on, regrets, the phone number of my childhood best friend that must ring somewhere else now (653-0417), regrets, a television jingle, the unprocessed mash of my brain. The men I've loved have appreciated that; not the timing maybe, but the show.

If I manage to fall back asleep, I sleep late. I'm exhausted, not yet ready to *face the day*, and the men I've loved—the ones who have been worth a damn—have let me sleep. Have slipped soundlessly out of the sheets and into the kitchen, where they pulled the eggs from the fridge, a frying pan from a cupboard and managed, somehow, to piece together their own damn breakfasts.

El present is a gift.

Josefina Báez

…**A** woman named City
Hips swing   male or female
We swing creating our **tale**
Male **or** female   we swing
No one to blame or complain   but **go**
Just **go** let go **go** slow go fast
But **go**
Crooked City   A woman named cupid
City   glorifying the finest brutality in **blue**
City   'nuestro canto con viva emoción'
City   'a la guerra a morir se lanzó'
Suerte que la 107 se **arrulla** con Pacheco
Pacheco tumbao añejo
Pacheco flauta   Pacheco su nuevo **tumbao**
El Maestro   El Artista   Tremendo Cache   compartido en Cruz   Juntos de nuevo como al detalle   Tres de **Café** y dos de **azucar**   Con el **swing** del tumbao y reculando como Ciguapa Me chulié en el hall…

This Moment of Mine

Marigloria Palma

Translated by Carina del Valle Schorske

I drink down my aspirins and watch the stars shiver.
This is my time, time of jet planes and plastic bombs.
Atomic era of the calculator. Ecological time,
biochemical time, transplant time, cancer time.

In a corner of the sky the tainted moon
(prostitute moon) puts her rabbits out to pasture
over her beaten breast. She passes, meditative, dragging
her swarm of wilted lilies, her dusty bitter God-help-you.

Man defiled her with his ideas (his scientific alchemy)
blasting rockets between her radiant hips and storming
her secret locks. Then he climbed up and spat in her face,
digging his heels in her chest. Brutalized moon

without mystery or shadow. Man has stripped you down
with his hands of clay. He's blackened you with his magic
machine of flame-for-brains. He's crushed your thighs
of foam and cream, your throat of milk, your transparent pubis.

But still you laugh, impassive, lifting your brow like a mad queen
on the eve of a coup… On earth the poet thinks of you and sobs:

don of words, genius of fine-wired syllables, he fashions you
a clever new snatch of blood and torment: a poem, sky-blue.

Este Momento Mío (de La noche y otras flores eléctricas)

Trago aspirinas y miro las estrellas parpadear.
Este es mi tiempo, tiempo de avión a chorro
y bomba plastic. Era de la calculadora
y fuerza atomica.
Tiempo de ecologia, de transplantes,
de cáncer y bioquimica.

Por un rincón del cielo la luna mancillada
(luna prostituida) pastorea sus conejos
con los senos vencidos. Pasa meditativa
arrastrando el enjambre de sus lirios ajados
y el Diostesalve polvoriento y ácido.

El hombre la ultrajó con sus ideas
(su cientifica alquimia) disparando cohetes
que ensuciaron sus radiantes caderas
y desentrorinzaron sus secretos invictos.
Despues subió hasta ella y le escupió la cara
Hundiéndole en el pecho los tacones.

Luna brutalizada sin misterio ni sombra.
Te ha desnudado el hombre con sus manos de arcilla.
Te ha mancillado el hombre con la maquina magica
De su ardiente cerebro. Ha estrujado tus muslos
De natilla espumosa, tu garganta de leche,
Tu transparente pubis.

Pero aun rielas impavida levantando la grente
Como una reina loca depronto destronada…
En la tierra el poeta te contempla y solloza
Y con don de palabras y alambritos de silabas
Te fabrica ingenioso una nueva vagina
Con su angustia y su sangre: un celeste poema.

Solitude

Marigloria Palma

Translated by Carina del Valle Schorske

My heartbox
refuge of the green shoot
avidly aiming towards
the quiet quake
of another melancholy…

In case just now
another shoot makes an echo.

Solitude.
Fountain of solitude;
soul on soul
sole death.
I'm with myself in my hour;
you in yours.
Us. Our death.

The whole black earth
shakes in wait
for the new harvets
of blonde angels.

My sleepless windows
peek out at the balcony of time
from behind the blinds.

Go away!
I want to look at myself.
To look at myself in my own light.
face to face, body to body
in iterations of windows
and I's, pulled along
by the hand of time.

Solitude!
Forgetting!
Solitude!

Bubbles…

Get out!

Soledad (from Canto de los olvidos)

Pecho mío,
refugio de una espiga
que apunta ávidamente
hacia el temblor callado
de otra melancolia…

Por si en este momento
otra espiga hace eco.

Soledad.
Fuente de soledad;
el alma con el alma:
muerte única.
Yo conmigo en mi hora;
tú contigo.
Nosotros: nuestra muerte.

Toda la tierra negra
se sacude y espera
a los angeles rubios
de la nueva cosecha.

Mis ventanas
con ojos desvelados
frente al balcón del tiempo
abren sus celosias.

Vete!
Quiero mirarme.

mirarme a luz mia;
de mi cara a mi cara;
cuerpo a cuerpo;
en multiplicaciones
de ventanas y yos,
arrastrada por la mano
del tiempo.

Soledad!
Olvido!
Soledad!
Burbujas…

Vete!

Intruder

Melanie Márquez Adams

What bothers me isn't so much the dread of becoming the punching bag for malicious gossip. No, that's not it. What terrifies me, what raises my pulse, is the thought of inspiring pity. I can just hear them, my neighbors, "It's never *too* late to find love, don't worry dear." "My cousin Mary got married at *forty-eight.* Can you believe it?" "Bless your heart. It's going to be *okay.*" No, I can't go through that. Not right now. I drag my feet to the sofa and plunge into surrender with a tired moan. Buried under the blanket, I long to drift away and escape from the world and my head. But before sleep comes to my rescue, I hear a thump on the glass.

A snout pressed against the glass door in my living room. So still that for a moment I think it must have died from the impact. I approach the door in a floating motion and knock on the glass with my fingertips. I hold my breath waiting for a reaction but it doesn't even flinch. I kneel down next to it and check its breathing. *The poor thing, is it really dea...* A wild jack-in-the-box startles me. I lose my balance and fall on my back. I raise my hands, forgetting for a terrifying instant the translucent barrier that separates us. Mortified, my self-pity unleashes. *Do you see? That is why he dumped you, because you are stupid. I crawl to the bedroom and attempt to make the bed. Why are you cleaning up? Why bother?* Shrugging, I stride across the room towards the kitchen. A moist chocolate cake—less than a half of it actually—splattered with cream in the fridge. I shoo the guilt away like flies. Who cares? No one left to judge me anymore. No one to look at me, disgust increasing in his beady, rodent-like eyes.

I gaze at the kitchen clock as if waiting for an oracle to send me off to my next mission. No such luck. Tick tock, taunting time. Eleven in the morning. I sit on the squeaky couch and turn on the television. *His* favorite news show blasts through. I am not in the mood for this morbid reportage he finds so fascinating. I explore dozens of stations, desperate to fill the dark menacing silence, finally landing on a ridiculous movie, where the heroine suffers and whines for over an hour until, right before the credits start parading across the screen, her problems—poof—disappear like a nauseating magic trick. To top it off, she manages to seduce a handsome millionaire and there they go, happily ever after into a rose-gold sunset. What a relief! No need to know what's happening with the nation or with the rest of the world anymore. No reason to stress about keeping up with his enlightened conversation, listening with undivided attention like a pathetic puppy.

I remain in the same spot until darkness sets in. The plate is now shining with grease, mourning the pastry that used to be. From the corner of my eyes, I catch a glimpse of the snout, spying. This time accompanied by a set of enormous glassy eyes. I stare at the creature and drag myself to the glass door to scare it away. I notice that half of my rose bushes are gone.

I could trap it, make it pay, finish it off. But it's all the same anyway. I don't have to keep a tidy garden anymore. Instead I make an obscene gesture and growl at the thing. Go ahead, wipe out the entire garden, just leave me the hell alone!

I haven't left the house for two days, I think. Inside, time remains still. The main event? The creature lurking through the glass door. Whenever the fatigue of not doing anything weighs on me, right before drifting away, I am certain *it* is looking at me. Same thing, as I slide into being awake. I know that the snout will be there, right on the same spot, haunting me, stalking me, annoying but honest, grotesque but real. A presence. Just like *he* was.

On the morning of day three I roll out of the sofa, hungry, craving something sweet. Desperate, I comb every corner of the kitchen, feeling the depths of the shelves and the fridge. Nothing. I panic. The convenience store is only two blocks away, but no, those nosy neighbors. I can't!

At first, I ignore it, hoping it will get tired. But the endless thumps stab my ears. Would you please just leave me alone you wicked beast! But it won't. The stubborn furry snout keeps at it: bump, bump, bump. Exhausted, I let the covers slide down my face.

I crouch down next to it. A gray mass of fur with long ears, whiskers protruding like silvery rays of moonlight. Its eyes, shiny black pearls. It looks at me.

I surrender to it.

For the first time in several days, I walk down the hall towards the front door. Standing so close to the world on the other side makes me dizzy, afraid. I look at the objects located in a dusty corner, next to the umbrella stand. A cheap basket overflowed with toys and trinkets of his dog. He left in such a hurry! That scumbag, abandoning his beloved Chihuahua's belongings. What an idiot!

I shake my head and rummage through the tiny items. A flashy collar emerges. I toss half of the basket's contents and find the matching fuchsia leash. The sparkling rhinestones hurt my eyes and I groan. I can still remember that day, when he bought the ludicrous set. Oh, how he ran home practically drooling to put it on his *baby*. That's how he referred to that horrendous animal. I laugh hysterically. I laugh until my cheeks ache, until my throat is sore.

I stretch out my body and go back to the living room. With my face relaxed from all the laughing, I exchange a conspiratorial look with my tiny intruder.

Why, hello there! It is so nice to finally meet you.

Fifteen minutes later, the rabbit and I walk down the street. The fuchsia leash sways cheerfully each time the spongy figure hops. A wave of whispers rises behind us, rippling through my body, tickling me. Yes, *they* stare at me, my astonished neighbors, but the looks are of surprise, disapproval. Fear. I do not catch even a tiniest glimpse of pity. Eagerly, I start thinking about the luscious cakes and sweets I will purchase. I will add to my shopping bag two bottles of wine, cheese, bread, and—why not?—some well-deserved fruits and vegetables for my new roommate.

Just five more hops and we will be at the store.

After Ocean

Norma Liliana Valdez

for México

& this is how we danced: shadows lifted
from the streets, late September turning our hunger

into plums, ripe in our palms. the cempazúchitl
were veils of gold. your whisper was night

through my hair—my hair, a river's current
we spelled our names in heartbeats & spilled ourselves

like bracken waters. when our lips did not touch, the moon
broke like rain clouds. in the echoes of her thunder

were splintered bones, limbs disjointed—
the body's inevitable unraveling. beneath our feet

splitting stones & another cumbia—another current
waxing. waning. time stood useless

motionless to our farewell. which is to say: I found
breath in you. which is to say:

the cenzontle's song had already left its body

Contributors

Li Yun Alvarado is the author of the chapbooks *Words or Water* and *Nuyorico, CA*. A poet and scholar, her work has appeared in *Wise Latinas: Writers on Higher Education*; *The Acentos Review*; *PMS Poemmemoirstory*; and *Cura: A Literary Magazine of Art and Action*, among others. She has served as the Senior Poetry Editor for *Kweli Journal* and is an alumna of VONA/Voices Writing Workshop and AROHO. Li Yun is a native New Yorker living in Long Beach, California who takes frequent trips to Salinas, Puerto Rico to visit la familia. www.liyunalvarado.com

Gessy Alvarez is founder and editor of the web journal, *Digging Through The Fat*. She shares her love of art and culture as well as some of her offbeat observations on her podcast, *Digging Through with Gessy Alvarez*. She writes stories, poems, and essays about the middle of things.Her prose has appeared in *Lunch Ticket*, *APT: Aforementioned Productions*, *Volume One Brooklyn*, *Entropy*, *Drunk Monkeys*, *Literary Orphans*, and other publications.

Josefina Báez (La Romana, Dominican Republic/New York). Storyteller, performer, writer, theatre director, educator, devotee. Founder and director of Ay Ombe Theatre (1986). Alchemist of creative life process: Performance Autology (creative process based on the autobiography and wellness of the doer). Books published: *Dominicanish*, *Comrade*,

Bliss ain't playing, *Dramaturgia I & II*, *Como la una/Como uma*, *Levente no. Yolayorkdominicanyork*, *De levente: 4 textos para teatro performance*, *Canto de plenitud*, *Latin In* (Antología de Autología), *As Is E'* (anthology) and *Why is my name Marysol?* (a children's book). www.josefinabaez.com

Sandra Cisneros is a Mexican-American novelist, poet, and short story writer. Her books include *The House on Mango Street*, *Caramelo*, and *Woman Hollering Creek*. She is the recipient of a fellowship from the National Endowment for the Arts as well as a Macarthur "Genius" Grant. She recently was granted an Art of Change Fellowship from the Ford Foundation.

Angie Cruz is editor of *Aster(ix)* and teaches creative writing in University of Pittsburgh. She published two novels, *Soledad* and *Let It Rain Coffee* and her third novel, *Dominicana,* is forthcoming.

Carina del Valle Schorske is a poet, essayist, and Spanish language translator at large in New York City. Her work has appeared at the *Los Angeles Review of Books*, *The New Yorker online*, *Lit Hub*, *The Point*, *The New York Times Magazine*, *The Offing*, *The Awl*, and elsewhere. She recently won Gulf Coast's 2016 Prize for her translations of the Puerto Rican poet Marigloria Palma. She is the happy recipient of fellowships from CantoMundo, the MacDowell Colony, Bread Loaf, and Columbia University, where she is a doctoral candidate in Comparative Literature. Find her @fluentmundo on Twitter.

Armando García is Assistant Professor of English at University of California, Riverside. He is completing his first book, *Impossible Indians: The Native Subjects of Decolonial Performance.*

Lizz Huerta is a working-class writer from the borderlands of Southern

California. Her work has appeared in *The Rumpus*, *Lumina*, *The Portland Review*, *Duende*, and other publications. She is currently polishing up a short story collection and fantasy novel. twitter @lizzhuerta.

Joe Jiménez is the author of *The Possibilities of Mud* (Korima 2014) and *Bloodline* (Arte Público 2016). Jiménez is the recipient of the 2016 Letras Latinas/ Red Hen Press Poetry Prize. Jimenez's essays and poems have appeared in *The Adroit Journal*, *Iron Horse*, *RHINO*, *Bat City*, and *Waxwing*, and on the PBS NewsHour and Lambda Literary sites. Jimenez was recently awarded a Lucas Artists Literary Artists Fellowship from 2017-2020. He lives in San Antonio, Texas, and is a member of the Macondo Writing Workshops. For more information, visit joejimenez.net.

Clarissa A. León is the managing editor for *Aster(ix) Journal* and a MFA nonfiction candidate at the University of Pittsburgh.

Melissa Lozada-Oliva is a poet & educator living in Brooklyn by way of Boston. She is the author of chapbooks rude girl is lonely girl! & peluda. Her work has been featured in *Remezcla*, *Buzzfeed*, *Glamour Magazine*, *Muzzle*, *Bustle*, *Huffington Post*, & *The Guardian*. She is currently an MFA candidate at NYU's Graduate Program for Creative Writing.

Melanie Márquez Adams traverses cultural and language borders as an Ecuadorian-American writer. She is the author of the short story collection, *Mariposas Negras [Black Butterflies]* (Eskeletra Editorial, 2017). Her work has appeared in *The Acentos Review*, *Thrice Fiction Magazine*, *Nagari Magazine*, *Literal: Latin American Voices Magazine*, *Six Words Fresh Off the Boat: Stories of Immigration, Identity, and Coming to America*, *ViceVersa Magazine*, and other publications. She is a Spanish instructor at East Tennessee State University. You can find her at melaniemarquezadams.com and @melmarquezadams.

Marigloria Palma was born Gloria María Pagán y Ferrer in 1915. Records differ regarding her birthplace—either Loiza or Canovanas, Puerto Rico—but she was raised by her working-class single mother before leaving school to work first as a maid and later as an assistant to a photographer in San Juan, the island's capital. In 1942, she was the second woman (after Julia de Burgos) to receive the island's premier poetry prize from the Institute of Culture. She cultivated a wide-ranging creative practice—folklore, children's literature, theater, poetry, fiction, drawing, and painting—over her fifty year career.

Adriana E. Ramírez is a PEN/Fusion award-winning nonfiction writer (2015, *Dead Boys*, Little A), storyteller, critic, and performance poet based in Pittsburgh. She co-founded *Aster(ix) Journal* with Angie Cruz. She is completing her next book, *The Violence*, due from Scribner in 2018. More information on her can be found at aeramirez.com.

Elizabeth Rodriguez Fielder is Assistant Professor of English at University of Pittsburgh. She is completing her first book *Unity of Art: Grassroots Cultural Activism of the Civil Rights Movement*.

Tanya Shirazi is a first-year M.F.A Fiction Candidate at the University of Pittsburgh.

Hecha en México, **Norma Liliana Valdez** made her way to California in her mother's pregnant belly. She is an alumna of the VONA/Voices Writing Workshop, the Writing Program at UC Berkeley Extension, and was a 2014 Hedgebrook writer-in-residence. She is the winner of the 2016 Tinderbox Poetry Journal prize with her poem "Tepoztlán

Blues," selected by Eduardo C. Corral. A member of the Macondo Writers' Workshop and a CantoMundo fellow, her poems appear in *Calyx*, *Huizache*, *Rio Grande Review*, and *Tinderbox Poetry Journal*, among others.

Angela Velez is an editor, writer, and second-year MFA Fiction candidate at the University of Pittsburgh.

Laura Winther Galaviz holds an MFA from Sarah Lawrence College. You can find her work in *Colorado Review*, *The Rumpus*, *Grist*, *The Common*, and elsewhere.

Acknowledgments

Melissa Lozada-Oliva

"Housecall" originally appeared in *Muzzle Magazine*

"Housecall" and "yosra strings off my mustache two days after the election in a harvard square bathroom" appear in *Peluda* (Button Poetry, 2017). Reprinted with permission from the author.

Josefina Báez

"The present is a gift." first appeared in *Dominicanish.*

Reprinted with permission from the author. *Dominicanish* is now in its 8th 'commutative law game' publication with photos by Giovanni Savino. Every time the text is published, its order and the highlighted text within is reorganized for the occasion.

Li Yun Alvarado

"Poe Park" first appeared in *PALABRA: A Magazine of Chicano & Literary Art.* Issue 4, 2008. Reprinted with permission from the author.

www.ingramcontent.com/pod-product-compliance
Lightning Source LLC
Chambersburg PA
CBHW062023190726
48284CB00014B/2633

* 9 7 8 1 9 4 2 5 4 7 0 8 2 *